# NUMBERS

## HOW TO WRESTLE WELL WHEN YOU'RE WORN OUT IN THE WAITING

Written by Marissa Henley and Kelley Brown
(c) 2022 by Proverbs 31 Ministries
All Scripture quotations are English Standard Version (ESV) unless otherwise noted.

# We must exchange WHISPERS with God before SHOUTS with the world.

LYSA TERKEURST

**PAIR YOUR STUDY GUIDE WITH THE FIRST 5 MOBILE APP!**

This study guide is designed to accompany your study of Scripture in the First 5 mobile app.

You can use it as a standalone study, or as an accompanying guide to the daily content within First 5.

First 5 is a free mobile app developed by Proverbs 31 Ministries to transform your daily time with God.

Go to the app store on your smartphone, download the First 5 app and create a free account!

WWW.FIRST5.ORG

# welcome to NUMBERS

When my two oldest children were younger, we lived in Indiana, 600 miles away from my hometown in Arkansas. Because of my husband's hectic work schedule and my strong desire for the kids to have time with their grandparents, I often made the long drive back to my hometown on my own with a preschooler and a toddler in the backseat.

In those days, we didn't have devices with streaming video. I placed a giant bag of toys on the passenger seat, and I'd try to ration them out between rest stops, handing back toys and then snacks whenever someone got fussy. When the toys ran out, I used a portable DVD player strapped to the back of my driver's seat headrest. I'd keep one hand on the steering wheel and reach back with the other hand. Without looking, I could push the right buttons to cue up a Bob the Builder video and enjoy a few minutes of calm.

The journey was long and difficult, but the promise of grandparents to help with the kids kept me going. I knew the destination would be worth it, but in the middle of Missouri, I would start to despair. I was tired, and the kids were cranky — there were hundreds of miles to go. It seemed like the wait to see the grandparents' smiling faces would never end.

The wait between the start of a journey and its promised end can be exhausting. Maybe you're worn out from waiting today. You're waiting for healing. You're waiting for a husband or for children. You're waiting for a relationship to be restored or for your diligence at work to be rewarded. You're tired of the difficulties you face as a Christian who's been redeemed but is still waiting for heaven.

As we dig into the story of Numbers, we'll find that we have so much in common with the wandering Israelites. They were stuck in the wilderness between their rescue from Egypt and their settlement in the promised land. During their long wait, they were tempted to grumble, doubt God's promises and disobey His commands. But God gave them the gifts of His presence, His provision and His mercy even when they repeatedly sinned against Him.

If you're struggling to wrestle well in your wait, I hope you'll find encouragement and comfort in the book of Numbers. As we read about God's care for the Israelites, we'll learn about God's care for us through His Son, Jesus Christ. We may be tempted to grumble, doubt and disobey, just as the Israelites did, but God has given us mercy and grace through the sacrificial death of Jesus. He's given us His indwelling presence through the gift of His Spirit. He's given us commands in His Word so we know how to serve and worship Him in a way that glorifies Him. God will not withhold anything we need as we wait in this wilderness for the consummation of our salvation — the day we see our Savior's face.

# INTRODUCTION

When someone mentions the book of Numbers, long lists of names and numbers probably come to mind. Numbers does contain numbers: for example, the two censuses in Numbers 1 and Numbers 26. However, the book of Numbers is primarily the narrative of the Israelites in the wilderness.

## WHAT IS NUMBERS ABOUT?

The name of the book of Numbers may give us the impression that we're back in algebra class. Its name originated in the Greek translation of the Old Testament, called the Septuagint. This translation named the book *Arithmoi*, which became *Numeri* in the Latin Vulgate translation and now *Numbers* in our English Bibles.[1]

However, the Hebrew names for this book describe the contents more accurately. Hebrew readers have referred to Numbers as "in the wilderness" or "the LORD spoke." These names come from the first verse of the book: *"**The LORD spoke** to Moses **in the wilderness** of Sinai, in the tent of meeting, on the first day of the second month, in the second year after they had come out of the land of Egypt …"* (Numbers 1:1, emphasis added). Both of these names reflect primary themes of the book: God's people were in the wilderness, and God was at work in their midst.[2]

## WHO WROTE NUMBERS?

The first five books of the Bible — Genesis, Exodus, Leviticus, Numbers and Deuteronomy — are also known as the Pentateuch. These books are historically attributed to Moses.

There are a few indications throughout the Pentateuch that Moses likely had the help of a scribe or editor: Deuteronomy narrates Moses' death, and Numbers describes Moses as the meekest man on earth. (Deuteronomy 34; Numbers 12:3) Moses probably didn't pen either of those remarks. However, we find evidence in the books themselves as well as in the New Testament that Moses was the primary author:

• Numbers 33:2, Deuteronomy 31:9 and Deuteronomy 31:24 mention Moses writing down God's law and aspects of the Israelites' journey from Egypt.[3]

• In a discussion with the Pharisees in Mark 10:2-5, Jesus attributed to Moses the writing of Deuteronomy 24.

• Jesus didn't correct the Sadducees' statement that Moses wrote the commandments, and Jesus referred to Exodus as *"the book of Moses"* (Mark 12:18-27).

• In Romans 10:5 and 2 Corinthians 3:15, the Apostle Paul also attributed to Moses the authorship of the law.

# TO NUMBERS

Whatever assistance Moses may have received in writing the Pentateuch, we can trust God's inspiration and preservation of His Word for us in our Bibles. Second Timothy 3:16 tells us that *"All Scripture is breathed out by God and profitable for teaching, for reproof, for correction, and for training in righteousness."* Numbers, along with all of the Old Testament, has been given to us by God to point us to His Son, Jesus Christ. Jesus Himself confirmed this when He explained the Old Testament to some disciples after His resurrection: *"And beginning with Moses and all the Prophets, he interpreted to them in all the Scriptures the things concerning himself"* (Luke 24:27).

## WHY SHOULD WE STUDY NUMBERS?

Knowing that Numbers is God's Word to us, we can expect to draw nearer to Him as we study it. Specifically, in the book of Numbers we will learn more about God's character as we see themes of holiness, sin, forgiveness, order and worship. We will see our sin more clearly as we read about the rebellious Israelites. We will understand Jesus' redemptive work for us more clearly as His role as our Mediator is foreshadowed by Moses and by Aaron, respectively Israel's first leader and first high priest.

Numbers is an important part of God's Word. It is quoted or referred to many times in both the Old and New Testaments, demonstrating its importance to the biblical writers. Let's look at a few highlights.

Psalm, the hymnbook of God's people, often reflects on God's miraculous work in bringing the Israelites out of Egypt and caring for them in the wilderness. In Psalm 78, the psalmist tells us to share these events with future generations. (Psalm 78:4) He describes how, as the book of Numbers reveals, the Israelites disobeyed God in the wilderness and forgot what He had done for them. (Psalm 78:9-20) Even in their unfaithfulness, God showed compassion and mercy. (Psalm 78:37-38)

In Psalm 95:8-11, we find a warning not to harden our hearts like the Israelites did in the wilderness. (Numbers 20:2-13) Psalm 106:12-13 recalls the wonders God did in bringing the people out of Egypt and how quickly they forgot His provision. (Numbers 11:4-6) After describing the ways the Israelites disobeyed God, the psalmist celebrates God's deliverance, compassion, steadfast love and covenant promises. (Psalm 106:43-45)

The New Testament also contains connections to Numbers. John shows how the serpent Moses held up in Numbers 21:8-9 points us to Jesus: *"And as Moses lifted up the serpent in the wilderness, so must the Son of Man be lifted up, that whoever believes in him may have eternal life"* (John 3:14-15). In 1 Corinthians 10:5-11, Paul warns us to learn from the example of the Israelites and not engage in sin, grumbling and testing God. Hebrews 3-4 compares the hardness of the Israelites' hearts with the hardness of the hearts of those who do not have faith in Christ.

We have so much to learn from the failures of the Israelites and from God's faithfulness in the midst of their faithlessness. When we're wrestling through our wait in the wilderness, we can draw from the principles and encouragement we'll find in Numbers. God has a purpose for each word in His Word. We can trust Him to use our study of Numbers to transform us and renew our minds. (Romans 12:2)

# NUMBERS AND THE STORY *of the Israelites*

AS WE BEGIN OUR STUDY, IT'S IMPORTANT TO GET OUR BEARINGS IN THE HISTORY OF THE ISRAELITES AND HOW NUMBERS FITS INTO THAT STORY.

## GENESIS

The story of Israel as God's chosen nation started in Genesis when God made promises to a man named Abraham. God promised Abraham that a great nation would come from him, that his descendants would be numerous and that God would give them the land of Canaan. (Genesis 12:2-3; Genesis 15:5-6; Genesis 17:1-8) Abraham had a son, Isaac, and Isaac had a son named Jacob.

In Genesis 35, God changed Jacob's name to Israel. Israel had 12 sons, whose descendants became the 12 tribes of Israel. God orchestrated the events of the lives of Israel and his sons to bring their families to Egypt.

## EXODUS

More than 400 years later, the Israelites had grown in number in Egypt and were oppressed as slaves. (Exodus 1) God called Moses to bring His people out of Egypt and lead them to the land God had promised to Abraham. God delivered them from Egypt (Exodus 15) and brought them into the wilderness to Mount Sinai.

At Mount Sinai, God gave Moses the law, and the people built the tabernacle according to God's commands. At the end of Exodus, Moses finished building the tabernacle at the foot of Mount Sinai *"in the first month in the second year"* after the Israelites left Egypt (Exodus 40:16-17).

## LEVITICUS

The book of Leviticus prepared the Israelites to obey God's law when they arrived in the promised land. It contains the ceremonial, civil and moral laws given by God to Moses when they spoke at the tabernacle and on Mount Sinai. (Leviticus 1:1; Leviticus 27:34)

There are a few chapters of narrative in Leviticus 8-10 about the consecration of Aaron and his sons as priests, and the deaths of Nadab and Abihu. Aside from those events, Leviticus serves as a pause in the storyline, beginning and ending with the Israelites at the foot of Mount Sinai.

## NUMBERS

Numbers begins in the same location, the tabernacle at the foot of Mount Sinai, one month after the conclusion of Exodus. (Numbers 1:1) Numbers covers the time from Mount Sinai until right before the Israelites went into the promised land.

In this book, we read about the preparations to leave Mount Sinai, the journey to the promised land, the Israelites' rebellion and the resulting 40 years of wandering in the wilderness. There are also chapters of law, mostly given to Moses by God in the plains of Moab near Jericho. (Numbers 36:13)

## DEUTERONOMY

Deuteronomy mirrors Leviticus as a book that contains very little narrative. It had been 40 years since God brought His people out of Egypt, and the new generation was at the bank of the Jordan, ready to cross from the wilderness to the promised land. (Deuteronomy 1:1-3) Moses spoke to the people and recounted the events since the Exodus and the law for this second generation.

Toward the end of the book, God renewed His covenant with the people; Joshua was appointed as the new leader, and Moses died. The Israelites were ready to enter the promised land under the leadership of Joshua.

# THEMES
# IN NUMBERS

Numbers is a true story about our faithful, forgiving God and His faithless, forgetful people.
Here are some themes we'll be exploring through our study of this book.

## God's Presence, Provision and Promises

God's presence set apart this large group of ex-slaves, Israel, from all the other nations on earth. (Exodus 33:16) In Exodus, the tabernacle was built and filled with God's glorious presence. Now the Israelites were to live as a God-centered community. As they journeyed toward the land God promised to Abraham, Isaac and Jacob, they were dependent on God to provide for them and keep His promises. Over and over again, God demonstrated that He is faithful, sovereign and powerful. He keeps all His promises and brings about His purposes for His people.

## Walking by Faith, Not by Sight

As we study the example of the Israelites, we see a people often focused on their circumstances rather than looking ahead with eyes of faith. Their failure to believe God's promises — despite His faithfulness — led to sin, grumbling, rebellion and despair. We can learn from their example and make a different choice: to *"walk by faith, not by sight"* (2 Corinthians 5:7; see also John 20:29). Faith in God's presence, provision and promises leads to obedience to His commands, and hope in His salvation.

## A Holy God and His Sinful People

The Israelites were a sinful people with a holy God dwelling in their midst. Their sin was a violation of their covenant with God and deserved death. While death was often a consequence for their disobedience, God showed mercy by not completely destroying His people. God also provided Moses as a mediator for the people and established the priesthood and the sacrificial system to atone for the people's sin. The repeated grumbling and rebellion of the people put God's forgiveness and faithfulness on display.

I hope, as we study Numbers together over the next several weeks, God will use His Word to show us more of His character, more of our sin and more of His merciful salvation in Christ. Numbers is the narrative of the Israelites in the wilderness, but it is also part of the bigger storyline of the Bible: that God calls sinners to belong to Him and saves them by His grace. Take a minute to pray and ask God to draw you closer to Him and deepen your understanding of His Word as a result of this study.

# What You Have To Look Forward To in This NUMBERS Study Guide

*In addition to the background information and daily questions for studying Numbers, we have included several elements to deepen your study along the way.*

## WEEKEND REFLECTIONS

We will wrap up each week with a reflection on the "big picture," themes and applications of what we read in Numbers that week. We'll also join together in prayer, asking God to humble our hearts, strengthen our faith in Him and continue to open our eyes to the truths of His Word.

## MAP OF THE PROMISED LAND

Take a look at the land God promised to His people as you study and reflect on His faithful fulfillment of that promise.

## TIMELINE OF NUMBERS

In this timeline you'll find a visual representation of Israel's journey, so you can see where the people went, when they went there and for how long as God's plan for His people unfolded.

## NUMBERS IN REVIEW

We've highlighted some essential facts to know about Numbers — who, what, when and where — for easy reference.

## IN CASE YOU WERE WONDERING

Wrapping up our study guide, you will find 10 verses from Numbers that maybe you have heard somewhere before. Our First 5 team has written a quick study on each verse to take you even deeper into the meaning, context or Hebrew origins. This is your chance to get into some fun details of Scripture and have an even richer understanding and appreciation of God's Word the next time you hear a verse used.

# MAJOR MOMENTS

## Week 1

NUMBERS 1:1-46 — God commanded Moses to take a census of the people.

NUMBERS 1:47-54 — The Levites were appointed to guard and care for the tabernacle.

NUMBERS 2 — God established the location of each tribe's camp around the tabernacle.

NUMBERS 3 — The Levites served the Lord in place of the firstborn males.

NUMBERS 4 — God prescribed responsibilities for each clan of the Levites.

## Week 2

NUMBERS 5 — God gave the Israelites ways to deal with guilt and uncleanness.

NUMBERS 6:1-21 — The Nazirite vow consecrated an Israelite for special holiness.

NUMBERS 6:22-27 — God gave Aaron words of blessing to speak to the people.

NUMBERS 7 — The people brought donations for ministry in the tabernacle.

NUMBERS 8 — Aaron set up the lampstands, and Moses consecrated the Levites.

## Week 3

NUMBERS 9 — The Israelites celebrated the Passover, and God guided them through the wilderness.

NUMBERS 10 — The Israelites set out from Mount Sinai.

NUMBERS 11 — God appointed elders to assist Moses and punished the grumbling Israelites.

NUMBERS 12 — Miriam was struck with leprosy when she and Aaron opposed Moses.

NUMBERS 13 — Twelve spies were sent to Canaan and returned with their report.

## Week 4

NUMBERS 14:1-19 — The Israelites responded to the spies' report with rebellion, and Moses interceded for the people.

NUMBERS 14:20-45 — God punished the Israelites with 40 years in the wilderness.

NUMBERS 15 – God gave the Israelites instructions about atonement for sin, the importance of obedience, and offerings in the promised land.

NUMBERS 16:1-35 — Korah led an uprising of 250 men against Moses and Aaron, and the rebellion ended in death.

NUMBERS 16:36-50 — Aaron's atonement for the people's sin stopped a deadly plague.

## Week 5

NUMBERS 17 — God confirmed Aaron's priesthood with a budding staff.

NUMBERS 18 — God explained the duties and privileges of priests and Levites.

NUMBERS 19 — God prescribed laws for purification.

NUMBERS 20 — The new generation of Israelites departed for Canaan, but Moses and Aaron would not enter the promised land.

NUMBERS 21 — Israel received their first victory over the Canaanites.

## Week 6

NUMBERS 22 — Balak summoned Balaam, a pagan seer, to curse Israel.

NUMBERS 23 — Balaam delivered his first and second oracles.

NUMBERS 24 — Balaam delivered his third oracle.

NUMBERS 25 — Israel turned from God to worship Baal.

NUMBERS 26 — God commanded Moses and Eleazar to take a census of Israel's new generation.

## Week 7

NUMBERS 27 — God commissioned Joshua to be Moses' successor.

NUMBERS 28 — God gave specific instructions about public sacrifices and offerings.

NUMBERS 29 — God continued to outline a calendar of public sacrifices and pertinent laws.

NUMBERS 30 — God taught Israel about the obligation of vows.

NUMBERS 31 — God declared vengeance on Midian.

## Week 8

NUMBERS 32 — The tribes of Reuben and Gad settled in Transjordan.

NUMBERS 33 — Moses recounted the stages of Israel's journey.

NUMBERS 34 — God outlined the boundaries of the land of Canaan.

NUMBERS 35 — The Levites were given some cities in which to live.

NUMBERS 36 — God instituted a marriage rule to preserve each tribe's inheritance.

WEEK ONE

# DAY 1

---

**MAJOR MOMENT**: God commanded Moses to take a census of the people.

The book of Numbers opens with information to help us get our bearings in the storyline of the Israelites. Read Numbers 1:1-3 and note the key details.

Who was speaking, and to whom was He speaking?

Where were God's people at this time?

When did this happen?

What instructions were given?

Let's not miss the significance of the opening words, *"The LORD spoke"* (Numbers 1:1). Even though we read this over and over again in the Bible, we need to remember this is no small event: the Creator and King of the universe spoke to man. Over 150 times in the book of Numbers, God communicated with His people.[1]

As Moses, Aaron and other leaders took the census God commanded, they used an important method. Look at the repeated phrases in Numbers 1:20-43. For each tribe, how were the people counted?

*"... their generations, by their _____ , by their _____ _____..."*

The Israelites were counted by families because Israel was a nation of connected families who were descended from the 12 sons (tribes) of Israel.[2] A person who belonged to a family that belonged to one of the tribes of Israel was proven to be a descendant of Abraham and an heir to the land God promised him. (Genesis 12:7)

The Israelites were counted by families for a specific purpose. Look at Numbers 1:20-43 again. Which of the people were counted?

" ... according to the number of names, from _____ _____ _____ and upward, every man _____ _____ _____ _____ _____ ..." (v. 26)

The people of God were preparing to go to battle for the promised land. Every adult male (except the Levites) was expected to fight together as the family of God.

Today we, too — both men and women, laypeople and church leaders, believers of all ages — are called to join God's family in a spiritual battle against the enemies of our heavenly Father.

Read Galatians 3:26-4:7.

What does Galatians 4:4-5 teach us about what God has done to bring us into His family?

What are some of the benefits of being part of God's family? (See Galatians 3:29 and Galatians 4:6-7.)

For the Israelites in Numbers and for us today, belonging to God's family comes with gracious gifts as well as responsibilities.

How does Paul, in Ephesians 6:10-18, describe the battle we're fighting as the family of God?

What can you do today to put on the armor of God and stand firm with your brothers and sisters in Christ? (Ephesians 6:13)

Paul makes it clear we aren't fighting a physical battle, but we are called to a spiritual battle fought with prayer, truth, faith and the Spirit. When we're worn out and still waiting for victory, we can remember we aren't fighting alone. We can have courage knowing we're redeemed children in God's worldwide family.

# DAY 2

MAJOR MOMENT: The Levites were appointed to guard and care for the tabernacle.

In the census of Numbers 1, one tribe was not included: the Levites. To understand why, let's look back in Exodus, where God set apart the Levites for a unique purpose. While Moses was on Mount Sinai talking with God, the Israelites rebelled by making and worshiping a golden calf. (Exodus 32:1-24) What happened next was critical for the Levites and their place in Israel.

> What role did the Levites play in this incident, (Exodus 32:25-28) and what did Moses say was the result? (Exodus 32:29)

Here in Numbers, we learn more about the Levites and their responsibilities during Israel's wilderness journey.

> According to Numbers 1:53, where did the Levites camp?

> Why did they camp there? What responsibilities did they fulfill that were different from the Israelites who were counted in the census?

One theme we will see throughout the book of Numbers is the contrast between God's holiness and the people's sinfulness. The Israelites had the glory of God dwelling in their midst in the tabernacle. (Exodus 40:34-38) However, the people were not safe to live in communion with their holy God because of the stain of sin.

In the garden of Eden, Adam and Eve once enjoyed full access to God's presence. God walked in the garden, but when Adam and Eve sinned, they hid from God in fear and shame. (Genesis 3:8-10) Adam and Eve were sent out of the garden, and humanity's communion with God was broken. (Genesis 3:22-24)

Later, when God brought the Israelites out of Egypt, there were boundaries around His holy presence. To learn more, read Exodus 19:9-14.

What do these verses give as the penalty for approaching God in an improper way? (vv. 12-13)

What similarities do you see between Exodus 19:9-14 and Numbers 1:47-54?

What do these instructions teach you about God's holiness?

In the Old Testament, the tabernacle, and later the temple, had restricted access. Even the Levite priests had to atone for their sins before they could draw near to the holiness of God. (For example, see Leviticus 16:6 and Leviticus 16:11.)

When Jesus died on the cross, He restored our fellowship with God. He took the penalty for our sin and made a way for us to be declared righteous in God's sight. Levites no longer guard access to God because we can enter clothed in Christ's righteousness. [3]

>Do you ever feel like you're not good enough to enjoy God's presence? In what ways have you tried to "clean yourself up" for God?

>Read Hebrews 10:19-22. What do we have now because of the blood of Jesus? What are we able to do?

The only way to approach God is to be clothed in the righteousness of Christ, which is freely given to us by God's grace. Write out Hebrews 4:16 and put it in a place where you'll see it often, as a reminder of what Jesus has done to restore your fellowship with God.

*"Let us then with confidence draw near to the throne of grace, that we may receive mercy and find grace to help in time of need."* (Hebrews 4:16)

# DAY 3

**MAJOR MOMENT**: God established the location of each tribe's camp around the tabernacle.

Numbers 2, along with Numbers 1:52-53, describes the arrangement of the Israelite camp and the order in which they would set out when they moved from one place to another. Read Numbers 1:52-2:34 and fill in the names of the tribes on the diagram below.

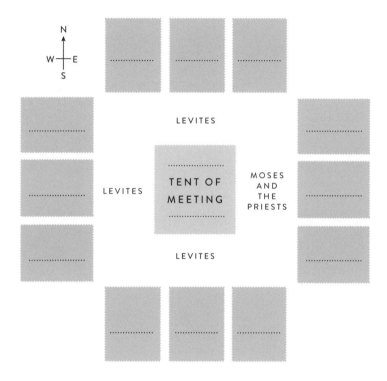

What was at the center of the camp? (Numbers 2:2) Which way would all the camps face?

Remember, as we discussed on Day 2 of our study, a few months earlier at Mount Sinai the people had rebelled and worshiped a golden calf. Read what happened next in Exodus 33:1-6.

What did God say about going with the people on their journey to the promised land? (v. 3) How did the people respond? (v. 4)

In Exodus 33:15-16, what did Moses plead with God to do, and why?

In Exodus 40:34-38, what do you learn about the tabernacle? How does this passage answer Moses's request in Exodus 33:15-16?

The Israelites forfeited the privilege of God's direct presence when they disobeyed God's law. However, God provided the tabernacle as a holy place and graciously accompanied His people through the wilderness. When we read about the tabernacle at the center of the camp, let's remember God's merciful forgiveness for the Israelites and also for sinners like you and me.

The centrality of the tabernacle also reminded the people of God's rightful place at the center of their lives and worship. As the people lived and journeyed in the wilderness, God's presence was to be at the core of their camp and their community.[4]

Our culture promotes self-centeredness, and sometimes others-centeredness, but rarely God-centeredness — unless, of course, we benefit in some way from having a spiritual life. But God's Word puts God at the center of everything. Not only for the sake of our spiritual, emotional or relational well-being but because God alone is worthy of being the focus of our attention, the center of our lives and the object of our praise and worship.

> If a stranger could observe your life for a week, including both your outward words and actions and your inner thoughts and prayers, what would he or she conclude is at the center of your life?

> List three practical steps you can take this week to have a more God-centered life. What needs to change in your thought life, on your phone, in the ways you spend your time or money, or in your approach to worship?

This is our motivation as we seek to live God-centered lives: that God loved us and sent His Son to save us and give us eternal life. (John 3:16) God-centered obedience doesn't earn our salvation, but it is our grateful response to the salvation we've been given in Christ.

# TIMELINE OF
# NUMBERS

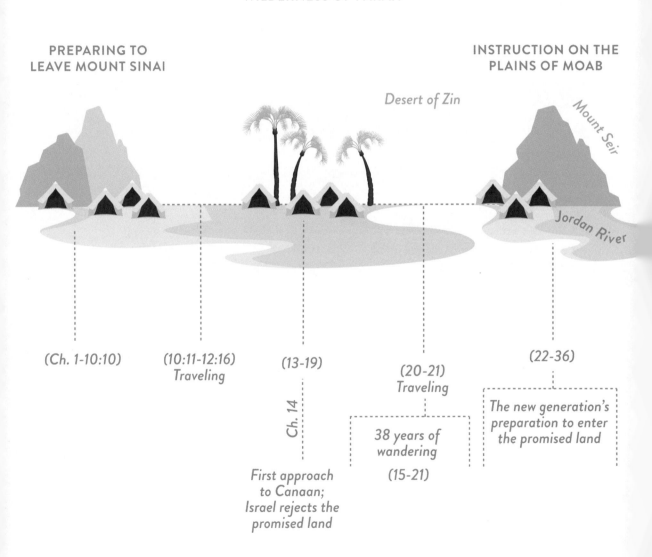

WILDERNESS OF PARAH

PREPARING TO
LEAVE MOUNT SINAI

INSTRUCTION ON THE
PLAINS OF MOAB

*Desert of Zin*

*Mount Seir*

*Jordan River*

*(Ch. 1-10:10)*

*(10:11-12:16)
Traveling*

*(13-19)*

*Ch. 14*

*(20-21)
Traveling*

*38 years of
wandering*

*(15-21)*

*(22-36)*

*The new generation's
preparation to enter
the promised land*

*First approach
to Canaan;
Israel rejects the
promised land*

# DAY 4

**MAJOR MOMENT**: The Levites served the Lord in place of the firstborn males.

In today's passage, we learn more about the Levites, their roles and their responsibilities. All Levite men served at the tabernacle, but only Aaron and his sons were appointed to serve as priests.

Read Numbers 3:4 as it recalls the event that happened in Leviticus 10:1-3.

What happened to Aaron's sons Nadab and Abihu?

What lesson do you think Aaron's other sons, Eleazar and Ithamar, learned from what happened to their brothers?

Now let's turn to Numbers 3:11-13.

The Levites were set apart by God for His service. In place of whom did God take the Levites?

Why did the firstborn males and firstborn livestock belong to the Lord? See Exodus 11:1-12:32 and Exodus 13:1 for helpful background.

Often in the Old Testament, we see a concept introduced that will be more fully developed and explained in the New Testament. Here we see the ideas of substitution and redemption. The Levites took the place of the other tribes' firstborn sons, who belonged to God. A redemption price had to be paid to the Lord — either with a Levite dedicated to service or with five shekels per head from each family. (Numbers 3:44-51) Throughout the generations, each Israelite mother would see her firstborn son at home and remember a Levite was serving in his place.[5]

Just as the Levites took the place of the firstborn males, Jesus Christ, *"the firstborn of all creation,"* took our place when He died on the cross (Colossians 1:15). He is our substitute, who purchased our redemption when He took the penalty our sin deserved.

Read the following verses and write down how they describe the work of Jesus as your substitute.

Romans 5:6-8

Romans 8:32

2 Corinthians 5:21

1 Peter 3:18

One day, we will all stand before the Lord's throne. We will either plead our case based on what we have done or we will point to the work of the only worthy substitute, Jesus Christ. Our good works will never be enough to meet God's standard of holiness. (Romans 3:23) Our only hope is in our Savior, who has fully paid the price of our redemption with His life, death and resurrection.

# DAY 5

**MAJOR MOMENT**: God prescribed responsibilities for each clan of the Levites.

After the summary of responsibilities in Numbers 3, more detailed descriptions are given in Numbers 4 for each of the three clans of Levites.

> Read Numbers 4:1-33 along with Numbers 3:21-37. Summarize the responsibilities of each of the clans of Levites below.
>
> Kohathites:
>
>
> Gershonites:
>
>
> Merarites:

Now, let's focus on Numbers 4:19, 4:27 and 4:33.

> What do you learn about the authority structure God put in place?

Looking at Numbers 4:34-49, especially verses 37, 41, 45 and 49, let's remind ourselves why Aaron and Moses were making these lists of Levites.

> Notice that this service was mandatory, not voluntary. From whom did these commands come? Who was the ultimate authority in the chain of command?

In the example of the Levites, we see how God appoints many individuals to serve Him and His people. No one person is asked to do it all. Everyone is given different responsibilities. Even those serving in the "inner circles" of ministry do so under the authority of others and ultimately under the authority of God.

We find a similar, though far greater, example of servant leadership in the life of Jesus. He came to serve sinners and lay down His life for them. (Mark 10:45; Philippians 2:7) In doing so, He submitted to the Father's will and focused exclusively on the Father's plan. (John 6:38)

As those who belong to Christ, we are also called to a life of service according to the gifts and opportunities God appoints to us.

> Read 1 Corinthians 12:4-6. What does Paul say about what makes us different and about what we have in common?

> Read Romans 12:3-8. What does Paul say in verse 6 about what we should do with our spiritual gifts?

What are some ways God has equipped you to serve Him and His Church?

Are you involved and serving in your local church? If so, ask the Lord to show you if there are new areas of service He's calling you to explore. If you're not connected to a church, what steps will you take this week to actively pursue a local church body where you can be ministered to and also minister to others?

# WEEKEND REFLECTION + PRAYER

This week we've seen that God is holy and deserves to be the center of our lives, but we are sinners who fail to give Him the worship and obedience He deserves. In His mercy, He sent His Son to bring us into His family, make a way for us to approach Him and secure our redemption as our substitute. Our grateful response as His redeemed children includes joining our brothers and sisters on the spiritual battlefield, pursuing God-centered obedience, and using our gifts to serve God and His people. As we continue our study of Numbers, I hope we'll deepen our understanding of what God has done for us in Christ and how we can respond to this gift in ways that glorify our Redeemer.

**PRAYER:** Gracious God, I praise You that You are a holy God who chose to make me part of Your family. Thank You for sending Jesus to be my substitute and redeem me from the penalty for my sin. By the power of Your Spirit, help me to grow in God-centered obedience, service and praise. In Jesus's name, amen.

# WEEK TWO

# DAY 6

---

**MAJOR MOMENT**: God gave the Israelites ways to deal with guilt and uncleanness.

In today's passage, we find laws related to uncleanness and guilt. Verses 1-4 deal with uncleanness, which refers to ceremonial impurity or imperfection, while verses 5-10 address the guilt of sin, or wrongdoing for which the people needed God's forgiveness. The rest of the chapter explains a procedure for discerning guilt or innocence.

In Numbers 5:2, what three reasons did God give to put someone outside the camp?

To be clear, God did not give this law out of disregard for those who were diseased or in mourning. Why did God give them this law? (Numbers 5:3)

What theological and public health reasons can you think of to explain why this would have been important?

In Numbers 5:5-10, God gave the people laws dealing with guilt caused by sin. God specified three actions that must be taken to atone for sin. Fill in the blanks below and identify these three actions.

Numbers 5:7: *"he shall _____ his sin that he has committed. And he shall make full _____ -for his wrong ..."*

Numbers 5:8: *" ... the restitution for wrong shall go to the LORD for the priest, in addition to the ram of _____ with which _____ is made for him."*

"Confession" involves admitting our sin openly to ourselves, God and others. "Restitution" refers to payment that is made to make things right after an offense is committed. "Atonement" describes the reconciliation or restoration of our relationship with God. In Old Testament law, restitution in human relationships and atonement to fix the sinner's relationship with God were closely connected.[1]

We have broken relationships with God and with others because of our sin. We can — and should — confess our sin honestly before God and others. We should do what we can to make things right when we've hurt someone. But in our relationship with God, the damage caused by sin is so great we could never do enough to atone for it.

Read Ephesians 5:2 and Colossians 1:20.

What did Jesus do to atone for your sin and reconcile you to God?

What does Ephesians 5:2 say about how we are to respond ("walk")?

The love and forgiveness we've received from God motivate us to walk in love with others. Because our relationship with God has been restored by His grace, we pursue reconciliation with others whenever possible.

Think of a time when your sin has caused damage to a relationship. Have you confessed your sin and received God's forgiveness? (1 John 1:9)

What steps do you need to take to pursue reconciliation with the person you sinned against?

Before we wrap up today's study, one note about the remainder of Numbers 5 (vv. 11-31). The "test for adultery" described in this passage may seem like a bizarre way to treat women; however, it demonstrates God's commitment to the sanctity of marriage and His care for women. Accusations of adultery were taken seriously by God's people. (Deuteronomy 22:22) This test described in Numbers 5 put justice in the hands of the righteous God who knows all things, protecting women from false accusations.[2] In this chapter dealing with uncleanness and guilt, the test for adultery reminds us again that God cares about justice and cares for His people.

# DAY 7

**MAJOR MOMENT**: The Nazirite vow consecrated an Israelite for special holiness.

While all of Israel was set apart as God's holy people, Numbers 6 describes a way for an Israelite to voluntarily make a commitment of special holiness for a period of time.[3] Those who took this vow served as a reminder of Israel's status as a nation set apart for God. (Exodus 19:5-6)[4]

Read Numbers 6:1-12. What were the three requirements of the Nazirite vow? (See verses 3, 5 and 6 in particular.)

Read Leviticus 10:8-9 and Leviticus 21:1-6. What connection do you see between the requirements for priests and the requirements for Nazirites?

According to Exodus 19:5-6, how would the Nazirites be a picture of what God called all of Israel to be?

Most of Numbers 6 focuses on ending a Nazirite vow. (vv. 9-21) Sometimes a vow ended because of unintentional defilement, (Numbers 6:9) and other times the declared time of separation came to an end. (Numbers 6:13) Numbers 6:9-12 provides for the fact that many well-intentioned Nazirites would fall short of keeping their commitments to holiness.

We don't make Nazirite vows today, but we may choose to set aside a time to fast from worldly pleasures and focus on the Lord in a more dedicated way. When we think of fasting, we may think of not eating. But we can also fast from certain beverages, social media, activities, or anything we're tempted to turn to instead of the Lord for comfort or satisfaction. Fasting is different from giving up sinful behavior, which involves repentance and permanent change. We may choose to temporarily fast from good things, such as food, to focus on that which is even better — the Lord.

Have you ever fasted for spiritual reasons? If so, what did you fast from and why? If not, what might you consider fasting from?

What things in your life cause you to struggle with distraction, overindulgence or misplaced priorities?

Is there anything God is asking you to give up for a while?

Personally, my string of broken New Year's resolutions is proof that I struggle to give up anything for more than a few days. Maybe you've seen this trend in your own life. Many of us have good intentions that end up being short-lived.

In a similar way, our struggles with spiritual fasting point to our need for the perfectly holy One.[5] Only Jesus lived a completely holy life for all of His days on earth. In response to the salvation we have in Him, we pursue holiness and consider setting aside times for fasting. God can use those fasts to grow our dependence on Him, much as He used Nazirite vows among the Israelites.

# DAY 8

---

MAJOR MOMENT: God gave Aaron words of blessing to speak to the people.

What comes to mind when you think of a blessing? Maybe you think of blessing your food before you eat. Maybe you think of people, experiences or material possessions as blessings from God. Maybe you're asking God to bless your efforts in your career, your home, your church or your community.

In Numbers 6:24-26, God shared words of blessing with Moses. This blessing was to be given by Israel's priests — Aaron and his sons. And although this blessing comes after the description of Nazirites in Numbers 6, it's important to notice that the blessing is for all of Israel. It would be spoken by the priests to the congregation of God's people, and God promised to bless the people in these ways. This blessing shows us what we most need from God.

Let's look at the first part of each verse: *"The LORD bless you ... the LORD make his face to shine upon you ... the LORD lift up his countenance upon you ..."* (Numbers 6:24-26).

In Hebrew poetry, certain structures are used regularly. In Numbers 6:24-26, we find synonymous parallelism, which means the first phrases in each of the three verses are saying the same thing in slightly different ways, and the second phrases are doing the same.

The Lord's "countenance" is His facial expression. These verses are saying that the Lord blesses us by turning His shining face on us.[6] Have you ever seen someone's face light up when they see you? That expression shows love, joy and delight.

> We may sometimes imagine God as a scowling judge or unhappy Father. What does this Numbers 6 blessing say about how God views His children?

> How does the love of God make a difference in your life?

Next, let's focus on the second phrases of each verse: *"... keep you ... and be gracious to you ... and give you peace"* (Numbers 6:24-26).

Read Psalm 121. How does this psalm enhance your understanding of what it means to be kept by the Lord?

In what specific way do you need the Lord to keep you today? Take your request to the Lord in prayer.

God's grace is His undeserved favor. Read Ephesians 2:8-9. How has God been gracious to you?

Read John 14:27 and Romans 5:1. How has God given you peace?

Blessing comes from the Lord, and He blesses us with gifts, such as His presence and His favor, that we receive by grace.

Read Galatians 3:13-14. How did Jesus make it possible for us to receive God's blessing?

Write a prayer of gratitude to God for His grace, love, peace and blessing that Jesus secured for you by enduring the curse of God in your place.

# DAY 9

---

**MAJOR MOMENT**: The people brought donations for ministry in the tabernacle.

Numbers 7 involves a jump back in time to Numbers 1. Before the census took place on the first day of the second month of the second year, the tribes of Israel brought gifts to the tabernacle in a 12-day procession of wagons, oxen, dishes and animals.

Numbers 7:1 mentions *"the day when Moses had finished setting up the tabernacle."*

> According to Exodus 40:16-17, when did Moses finish the tabernacle? How does this relate to the date mentioned in Numbers 1:1?

Read Numbers 7:1-9. Remember that on Day 5 we studied the three clans of Levites and their responsibilities.

> Why do you think Moses divided the six wagons and 12 oxen between the clans of Levites in the way described in Numbers 7:7-9? (Keep in mind what each clan was responsible for transporting from place to place.)

> When you consider their responsibilities and the fact that the Israelites were traveling to the promised land, how do you think the Gershonites and Merarites would have viewed these gifts from their fellow Israelites?

Who do you know who is serving God in ministry? How can you encourage them by meeting a practical need or showing your appreciation?

We find a lot of repetition in Numbers 7:12-83, along with the summary in Numbers 7:84-88. Using the first description of gifts from the tribe of Judah as an example, fill in the blanks to note the different ways these gifts would be used:

> "And his offering was one silver plate whose weight was 130 shekels, one silver basin of 70 shekels, according to the shekel of the sanctuary, both of them full of fine flour mixed with oil for a _____ _____; one golden dish of 10 shekels, full of _____; one bull from the herd, one ram, one male lamb a year old, for a _____ _____; one male goat for a _____ _____; and for the sacrifice of _____ _____, two oxen, five rams, five male goats, and five male lambs a year old."
> (Numbers 7:13-17a)

All the Israelites were involved in equipping the tabernacle and the Levites for the work and worship God had commanded. The gifts they brought demonstrated their understanding of the tabernacle's purpose. It was where God's people would worship Him with sacrifices according to His instructions.

When we come to worship today, we don't bring livestock or grain. We come with other contributions: voices ready to sing, hearts to serve, money to give, arms to reach out and comfort others, and hands to fold in prayers of praise and intercession.

Take a look at Romans 12:1 and Hebrews 13:15-16.

How can you offer an acceptable sacrifice to God today?

How do you currently contribute to your local church, financially or in other ways? How could you consider a new or increased contribution?

# DAY 10

---

**MAJOR MOMENT**: Aaron set up the lampstands, and Moses consecrated the Levites.

After the 12 tribes brought their contributions in Numbers 7, we read about the final preparations for worship in the tabernacle in Numbers 8. The end of this chapter describes how the Levites were consecrated *"as a gift to Aaron and his sons from among the people of Israel, to do the service for the people of Israel at the tent of meeting"* (Numbers 8:19).

But first, the Lord gave Moses instructions for Aaron regarding the lampstand in the tabernacle.

> Read Exodus 25:31-40. Which details about the lampstand are repeated in Numbers 8:1-4?

> What other details from Exodus 25 stand out to you?

When the tabernacle was built, Moses set up the lampstand opposite the table that held the Bread of Presence. (Exodus 40:24-25) This table held 12 loaves of bread that represented the 12 tribes of Israel and God's provision for them. (Leviticus 24:5-9)[7] When Aaron set up the lamps according to God's instructions, the lamps shone on the 12 loaves.

The Hebrew verb translated *"give light"* in Numbers 8:2 is the same verb used in the blessing of Numbers 6:25: *"the LORD make his face to **shine** upon you"* (emphasis added).[8] This light shining on the 12 loaves represented God's covenantal love shining on His people.

From Genesis to Revelation, light and darkness are important themes in the Bible. In the beginning, there was darkness until God said, *"Let there be light"* (Genesis 1:3). We will read in tomorrow's passage that God's presence guided the people through the wilderness as a cloud by day and fire by night — once again, a light shining in the darkness.

This theme carries through to the New Testament and Jesus' birth.

41

Read John 1:4-5 and John 8:12. What do you learn about Jesus as the Light of the world? What power does His light have?

Jesus is the Light of the world who calls His people to be lights in the world.

Read 2 Corinthians 4:4-6. What does verse 6 say about how we receive God's light? What is this light we receive?

Read Matthew 5:14-16. What is the purpose of letting the light of Christ in us shine?

Who do you know who is walking in darkness? How can you share the light God has shone into your heart with those who do not know Him?

When we feel stuck in darkness and weary of waiting for the light, we can remember that when Jesus returns, His light will shine even more brightly. There will be no darkness in the new heavens and new earth: *"And night will be no more. They will need no light of lamp or sun, for the Lord God will be their light, and they will reign forever and ever"* (Revelation 22:5).

# WEEKEND REFLECTION + PRAYER

This week we've learned more about what it means to be part of the redeemed family of God. Believers in Christ have been reconciled to God by Jesus' atoning sacrifice, so we pursue reconciliation with others. We've been given a Savior who was perfectly holy, so we pursue holiness. We've received undeserved blessings from God, so we offer sacrifices of time, money and worship to Him. We've been brought out of darkness and into His light, so we shine as lights to point others to His glory and grace. In our times of waiting and wandering, we wrestle as redeemed, reconciled worshippers living in the light of God's salvation.

**PRAYER:** Heavenly Father, thank You for the blessings of Your presence, steadfast love and salvation through Your Son. I confess that I am distracted, forgetful and too often content with darkness. Give me the courage to pursue holiness and shine as a light, that others may see the truth of who You are and what You have done for me. In Jesus' name, amen.

# WEEK THREE

NUMBERS

---

**MAJOR MOMENT:** The Israelites celebrated the Passover, and God guided them through the wilderness.

As we saw on Day 9, Old Testament narrative isn't always presented chronologically. As we study, it's important to notice the clues that help us sort out a timeline of connections with other passages of Scripture.

In the blanks below, write the event that occurred in each passage to create a timeline of the first two months of the second year after the Israelites left Egypt. (There's an answer key at the end of this study guide if you'd like to check your answers!)

| FIRST MONTH OF THE SECOND YEAR | | SECOND MONTH OF THE SECOND YEAR | |
|---|---|---|---|
| First day of the month | 14th day of the month | First day of the month | 14th day of the month |
| Exodus 40:16-17 | Numbers 9:1-5 | Numbers 1:1-2 | Numbers 9:9-11 |
| _____ | | | |
| Numbers 7:1-3 | | | |
| _____ | _____ | _____ | _____ |
| Numbers 9:15 | | | |
| _____ | | | |

The command to keep the Passover was given about a year earlier, right before the Israelites' exodus from Egypt. Read Numbers 9:1-14 with Exodus 12:1-20.

What did the people do to keep the Passover according to God's commands in Exodus 12:17-20?

What did the feast commemorate?

When was Passover observed?

Read John 1:29 and 1 Peter 1:18-19.

What connections do you find between the Passover and Jesus' sacrifice for us?

Now let's study Numbers 9:15-23 with Exodus 13:17-21, keeping in mind that Exodus 13 records Israel's flight from Egypt before Numbers 9.

When did the pillar of cloud and fire first appear with the Israelites? (Exodus 13:21)

Why do you think it's significant that the cloud of God's presence covered the tabernacle (Numbers 9:15-16) rather than resting somewhere else in the camp?

What practical purpose did the cloud serve for the Israelites? (Numbers 9:17-19)

Numbers 9:22 tells us that the people camped in one place as long as the cloud stayed over the tabernacle, *"Whether it was two days, or a month, or a longer time."* An occasional break from their journey probably would have been welcome, but as days turned into weeks or months, I wonder if they started getting restless. The promised land was waiting for them, after all, and they were still in the wilderness. They must have often wondered about God's seemingly erratic timing.

The same is true for us when we're stuck in a season of waiting and don't understand God's timing. Maybe you're ready to move, but God says, *Wait.* Maybe you're struggling to trust Him or discern how He's guiding you.

The same God who gave His Son to be the sacrificial Lamb also gave you His Spirit to dwell in you. He will never leave you nor forsake you. (Hebrews 13:5) His timing is often hard to understand, but it is always perfectly rooted in His wisdom and faithfulness.

Has there been a time when you were waiting and didn't understand God's timing? How did you handle the situation?

What truth about God from today's passages helps you to trust Him when you're worn out in the waiting?

# DAY 12

---

**MAJOR MOMENT**: The Israelites set out from Mount Sinai.

After almost a year since they arrived at Mount Sinai, the big moment arrived — the cloud lifted from over the tabernacle, and the people set out. (Numbers 10:11) God's people started their journey toward the promised land. Chapters 10-12 of Numbers describe the Israelites' travels from Sinai to Kadesh, in the wilderness of Paran.

Before they set out, God instructed Moses to make two silver trumpets. Read Numbers 10:1-10.

> List several purposes these trumpets served in the civil and religious life of the people.

Trumpets are used elsewhere in the Bible to point to God's judgment on His enemies and His triumph over them. In Joshua 6, the priests blew trumpets as the Israelites walked around the city, and the walls of Jericho fell. In the book of Revelation, John prophesies that seven trumpets will be blown. The first six will signal judgments God sends on the earth. (Revelation 8-9) The seventh trumpet will herald God's victory over the world. (Revelation 11:15-19)

In this passage we see the relationship between divine sovereignty and human responsibility. God was leading and guiding His people, and He would be victorious over His enemies. And yet the people also bore responsibility along the journey. They were to obey God's commands and fight when told to do so. They were to set out according to the cloud's movement and set out under the direction of Moses and the leaders of each tribe.

> Read Numbers 10:29-32. Why did Moses say he wanted Hobab to go with them when they set out from the wilderness of Sinai?

> Read Numbers 10:33-34. What did the ark do as it went before the traveling Israelites?

In each of these passages, humans were presented with choices and duties. But at the same time, God was clearly orchestrating the events according to His promises and plans.

How do you see the relationship between God's sovereignty and human responsibility in these verses?

As God sovereignly works to bring about His purposes, He often involves people in that work. We pray. We share the gospel. We serve the Church. But it is who God changes hearts and lives, draws sinners to Himself and uses His Church to minister to His people.

Read Philippians 2:12-13.

In what ways do you need to grow in holiness and obedience, bearing the fruit of your salvation?

In what ways do you see God at work in your life for His pleasure and glory?

When we're waiting for a difficult situation to resolve, we often feel the tension between divine sovereignty and human responsibility. We might wonder if we should keep waiting for God to intervene or if we have a responsibility to act. There's not an easy answer to this question ... but we can seek God's wisdom in prayer.

Are you waiting for God and wondering whether you should keep waiting or take action? Write the words of James 1:5 below and seek the Lord's guidance by bringing the situation to Him in prayer.

# DAY 13

MAJOR MOMENT: God appointed elders to assist Moses and punished the grumbling Israelites.

We'll read over the next few days that the journey of the Israelites from Sinai to Paran was marked by repeated cycles of the people's grumbling and the Lord's judgment. In Numbers 11, we read two incidents, one involving the complaints of the people at Taberah (vv. 1-3) and one at Kibroth-hattaavah. (vv. 31-34)

How did the grumbling in Numbers 11 begin? To what extent did the grumbling spread through the camp?

What were the people complaining about? (See verses 1 and 4-6.)

In what ways were their memories of Egypt inaccurate? (Compare their memories in Numbers 11:4-6 and the historical facts in Exodus 1:8-22.)

List the ways God responded to the people's grumbling in this chapter.

What does the Lord's judgment in Numbers 11 teach you about how He views grumbling and complaining?

When we're worn out in the waiting, we may be tempted to complain. But all our complaining is complaining against God. He is our Provider, our Sustainer and our Redeemer. When we complain, we reject His good plans for us. We ignore His gracious provision. We question His steadfast love and faithfulness.

Not only did the Israelites focus on distorted views of their past, but they also failed to thank God for His daily provision of manna. We may wonder how they could have gathered God's gift of miraculous food six mornings a week and still grumbled and complained against Him. But if we're honest, we know we often act just like them.

Thankfully, Scripture tells us that, rather than complaining against God, we can wrestle well in our waiting by crying out to God for help.

In the psalms, we find many examples of people crying out to God. David wrote Psalm 142 while hiding in a cave. (1 Samuel 22:1) He was being chased by King Saul and feared for his life. God had promised that David would become king of Israel, but David was still waiting for that promise to be fulfilled.

Read Psalm 142:1-7.

How is David's cry for help different from a complaint against God?

What are you tempted to complain about? In what ways might you be denying God's goodness and faithfulness with your complaints?

How can you change your complaints into cries for help from your heavenly Father?

When we cry out for help and wait for God's answer, we can have confidence God will hear us: *"But as for me, I will look to the LORD; I will wait for the God of my salvation; my God will hear me"* (Micah 7:7).

---

**MAJOR MOMENT:** Miriam was struck with leprosy when she and Aaron opposed Moses.

The next episode of grumbling involves a struggle most of us have experienced at some point either as a child or as a parent: sibling rivalry. Those who are closest to us are the most likely to get on our nerves, and our response is too often complaining or quarreling. Even Moses had to deal with the grumbles of his brother Aaron and sister Miriam.

Read Numbers 12:1-3.

What complaints did Miriam and Aaron have against Moses?

Why do you think the detail about Moses's meekness was included in Numbers 12:3? How does it help us understand the conflict in these verses?

In Matthew 12:34b, Jesus said, *"For out of the abundance of the heart the mouth speaks."* What do the words of Aaron and Miriam reveal about their hearts' attitudes toward Moses and his role compared to their roles in leadership?

Think about the last time you complained about another person. What did your complaints reveal about your heart?

Read Numbers 12:4-15.

What was God's response to Aaron and Miriam?

What did God say was unique about Moses as a prophet? (vv. 7-8)

We aren't told exactly why Miriam and Aaron started speaking against Moses at this point in the Israelites' journey. The appointment of the 70 elders in Numbers 11 may have made Miriam and Aaron feel their power was being threatened.[1] Regardless of the reason, it's important to realize Miriam and Aaron weren't simply complaining about their brother. They were questioning the way God chose to speak uniquely through His servant Moses. They were rebelling against God and failing to submit to His Word.

God said Moses was *"faithful in all my house"* (Numbers 12:7b). But Hebrews 1:1-2 and Hebrews 3:1-6 remind us that even Moses, used mightily by God, wasn't the sinless Chosen One.

How does the Hebrews passage describe the faithfulness of Moses compared to the faithfulness of Christ?

How do these passages compare the way God spoke in the past and the way God has spoken now?

God's judgment of Miriam demonstrated the seriousness of her complaints against Moses and against the giving of God's Word through him. Our grumbling against God's Word is just as serious now that God has spoken through His Son, Jesus Christ. As one commentator says, "To speak against the Scripture is to speak against the authority that God himself has instituted."[2]

What is your attitude toward the Bible? In what areas do you find it difficult to submit to the authority of God's Word?

Confess your struggles to the Lord, and ask for His help — and praise Him that *"there is therefore now no condemnation for those who are in Christ Jesus"* (Romans 8:1).

---

**M A J O R   M O M E N T**: Twelve spies were sent to Canaan and returned with their report.

Our study this week ends with a cliffhanger. The Israelites traveled through the wilderness and were in a position to scout out the promised land. The Lord commanded them to send out 12 spies, (Numbers 13:1) and when the spies returned with their report, Israel had a choice to make. Would they believe the promises of God or the majority report of fearful leaders? Next week, we'll read about their decision and its implications. But today, let's look at the promises of God and the work of the 12 spies.

God's words to Moses framed the work of the spies within the certainty of God's promise. Fill in the blanks with the reminder God gave Moses about God's purpose for the land of Canaan:

*"Send men to spy out the land of Canaan, which _____ _____ _____ to the people of Israel ..."*
(Numbers 13:2a)

Read Exodus 3:16-17. When they were still enslaved in Egypt, what had God promised to do for the Israelites?

How had God already kept part of that promise prior to these events in Numbers 13? (Hint: Ask Pharaoh in Exodus 14 ...)

God repeatedly told the people He was keeping His covenant with Abraham by giving Abraham's descendants the land of Canaan. His deliverance of the Israelites from Egypt and the way He was leading them toward the promised land should have fortified the people's confidence. The scouting mission into Canaan was meant to further strengthen the Israelites' faith in God's promises.[3]

But what did the spies (except for Caleb and Joshua) tell the congregation about Canaan? (Numbers 13:26-33)

What details about Canaan in their report actually proved that God's promise in Exodus 3:16-17 was true?

On the other hand, what news did they bring that seemed to contradict God's promise?

How do you think you would have felt as an Israelite who had been waiting for the promised land and now heard this report from the spies?

The Israelites who heard this report had two options. They could choose to remember God's past faithfulness and promises, or they could focus on their present fears and could doubt God's promise-keeping ability. When we face situations that seem impossible, we have the same choice to make.

Describe a time in your past when God was faithful to keep one of the promises in His Word. How did you see Him at work in your situation?

What are you afraid of today? What promise from God's Word can you cling to with confidence that God is at work in your situation? (If you need help finding a promise, check out some of these passages: Joshua 1:9; Psalm 23; Lamentations 3:21-24; Isaiah 43:1-2; Romans 8:38-39; Philippians 4:6-7.)

What practical step can you take to keep your focus on God's faithfulness rather than your fears?

# WEEKEND REFLECTION + PRAYER

As we continue studying the Israelites' wilderness years, we will see how their grumbling became a recurring theme. Imagine the wonders they had experienced — God even brought them through the sea on dry land to escape the Egyptian army! (Exodus 14) And yet they repeatedly questioned God's goodness and faithfulness by grumbling against Him and His provision.

We are no different from the complaining Israelites. We've experienced the wonders of His love and mercy — God sent His Son to be our Passover Lamb, who was sacrificed to rescue us from sin and death. And yet we question His goodness and faithfulness by grumbling against Him and His provision. Let's take some time today to examine our hearts, confess our sin and consider ways we can exchange our grumbling for gratitude.

**PRAYER:** Gracious God, You've been so good to me, and You've promised blessings — in heaven with You forever — beyond my wildest dreams. When I'm tempted to complain, help me to recognize my grumbling as grumbling against You. Help me to grow in gratitude for all You've done and to trust Your continued provision for me in Christ. In Jesus' name, amen.

WEEK FOUR

NUMBERS

# DAY 16

**MAJOR MOMENT:** The Israelites responded to the spies' report with rebellion, and Moses interceded for the people.

In today's reading, we find the fallout from the unfavorable report given by 10 of the 12 spies who scouted out the promised land. When Israel responded unfaithfully to the report, Moses interceded for the people and asked God to forgive them.

From Numbers 14:1-4, list three ways the Israelites responded to the report of the spies.

From Numbers 14:5-10, how did Moses, Aaron, Joshua and Caleb respond?

The distraught response of the Israelites ran deeper than tears and questions. Their desire to return to Egypt was a desire to reverse God's redemptive work in bringing them out of Egypt. (Numbers 14:2)[1] They focused on what their eyes could see rather than the promises of God. Their choice led to fear, grumbling and rebellion.

In contrast, Joshua and Caleb modeled trust in God's promises. They were not afraid because they remembered God's deliverance and had hope in God's protection and presence with them. (Numbers 14:6-9)

When was a time you faced a difficult situation and responded like the Israelites, with unbelief that led to rebellion, grumbling, fear or despair?

When was a time you faced a difficult situation and responded like Joshua and Caleb, with trust in God's promises that led to hope and peace? Or how could you respond this way in a situation you're facing now?

Imagine you are one of the angry Israelites, talking about stoning Moses and Aaron, when the glory of the Lord appears to all the people of Israel. (Numbers 14:10) What do you think you would be thinking and feeling in this moment?

Rather than jumping at the chance to start over with a new nation, Moses interceded for the Israelites. Intercession means the "act of intervening or mediating between different parties, particularly the act of praying to God on behalf of another person."[2] We read Moses's prayer of intercession in Numbers 14:13-19.

Read Exodus 34:5-7. Where did Moses get the description of God's character that he spoke back to God in Numbers 14:18?

How many attributes of God can you find in Moses's prayer of intercession? List them here. (God's attributes are His characteristics, such as goodness and love.)

In the New Testament, we learn that one of the many benefits we receive in Christ is that He intercedes for us. When our Savior pleads our case before the Father, He pleads on the basis of what He has accomplished: His perfect obedience and atoning, sacrificial death.

Read the verses below and write down the benefits you receive from the intercession of Christ.

Romans 8:34

Hebrews 7:25

1 John 2:1

When we face trials or challenges, we have a choice to make between faith and unbelief. We won't always trust God perfectly. We will sometimes struggle with doubt and fall short of the wholehearted confidence our trustworthy God deserves. But as 1 John 2:1 says, when we sin, we have a righteous advocate, Jesus Christ. Praise God that we have a Savior who knows our weakness and intercedes for us!

# DAY 17

---

**MAJOR MOMENT**: God punished the Israelites with 40 years in the wilderness.

After Moses interceded for the people, God responded by saying, *"I have pardoned, according to your word"* (Numbers 14:20). In His mercy, God did not immediately destroy all the people — but there were devastating consequences for their rebellion.

What was at the root of the Israelites' sin against God? Fill in the blanks below.

Numbers 14:11: *"And the LORD said to Moses, 'How long will this people _____ _____? And how long will they _____ _____ in me, in spite of all the signs that I have done among them?'"*

Numbers 14:23b: *"And none of those who _____ _____ shall see it."*

What does it mean to "despise" someone or something? In what ways do all sins come from despising God?

What were the consequences of the Israelites' rebellion ...

For the Israelites ages 20 and older? (vv. 29-30)

For their children? (vv. 31, 33-34)

For the 10 spies who brought the bad report? (vv. 36-38)

64

What did the Israelites do after hearing the consequences of their unbelief? Based on their actions, what do you learn about the genuineness of their repentance? (Numbers 14:39-45)

Our God is a just God who can't let sin go unpunished.

Read Romans 6:23 and James 1:14-15. What do you think it means that the *"wages of sin is death"*?

How have you seen sin leading to death in your life and in the world around you?

Even though our sin deserves death, Romans 6:23 ends with the good news of the gospel: *"For the wages of sin is death, but the free gift of God is eternal life in Christ Jesus our Lord."* On the cross, Jesus endured the wages of sin and died in the place of sinners: you and me. Our God is a merciful God who sent His Son to take the punishment we deserve for our doubt, faithlessness, unbelief and rebellion.[3]

For those who repent and turn to Christ, God forgives our sin and promises an eternal home with Him in heaven. (Romans 8:1; John 3:16) While we experience temporary consequences for sin and the painful reality of our fallen world, we can remember that we will not wander in the wilderness forever. We have a permanent, eternal home waiting for us. We will enter it not based on our own merit but because of the sacrifice our Savior made for us.

---

MAJOR MOMENT: God gave the Israelites instructions about atonement for sin, the importance of obedience, and offerings in the promised land.

Today's passage breaks from the narrative to describe offerings, sacrifices for unintentional sin, and laws regarding intentional defiant sin. This chapter may seem out of place following the momentous occasion of disbelief and judgment that came before it; however, as ancient Israelites read the book of Numbers, they would have found comfort in these words.

Despite the Israelites' repeated disobedience in Numbers 14, the instructions in Numbers 15 confirmed that God would eventually bring His people into the promised land. (Numbers 15:2; Numbers 15:17) He would continue to have a relationship with His people and bless them with abundant food and wine from which to make the offerings described here.[4] The relationship was broken but not destroyed.[5]

Numbers 15:1-21 describes offerings of grain, wine, animals and dough to be given to the Lord in the promised land. These offerings were not meant to atone for sin but to express the relationship between God and His people as that of a faithful Provider and His grateful children.

Read 2 Corinthians 9:6-8. What has God given to you in abundance?

How can you generously give from what you have received?

Numbers 15:22-36 describes two scenarios: unintentional sin and sin *"with a high hand"* (Numbers 15:30), which refers to defiant, deliberate, unrepentant sin. The example of the Sabbath-breaker in Numbers 15:32-36 was likely given as a practical example of the defiant sin described in Numbers 15:30-31.[6]

Read Numbers 15:30-31 with Hebrews 10:26-29.

How do these passages describe the defiant sinner's attitude toward God?

How is this defiant sin different from when a repentant believer struggles with sin?

Another New Testament passage tells us more about sin and forgiveness: 1 John 1:9-10.

How do you see a contrast between the repentant and the unrepentant sinner in these verses?

What does God promise to repentant sinners?

Read Numbers 15:37-41.

What were the tassels meant to help the Israelites remember?

Digging into a couple of the words in Numbers 15:39 will deepen our understanding of this passage. We may be surprised to find language like *"your own eyes, which you ... whore after,"* but this strong language reminds us of the seriousness of sin. The Israelites were joined to God in a covenantal relationship, but they were tempted to be unfaithful to the Lord.

The Hebrew verb for "to follow" (when Numbers 15:39 says *"not to follow after your own heart"*) can mean either to follow or to spy.[7] Readers were meant to remember the 10 spies who followed what their eyes saw — giants in the promised land — rather than remembering God's promises and commandments.

> Read Colossians 3:1-2. When you're tempted to be afraid of what you see or to chase after the treasures of this world, what are some practical ways you can remember to *"set your mind on things that are above"*?

# DAY 19

**MAJOR MOMENT:** Korah led an uprising of 250 men against Moses and Aaron, and the rebellion ended in death.

Numbers 16 describes the continued rebellion of the Israelites. A well-organized confrontation ended with the dramatic deaths of those who came against Moses and Aaron.

Read Numbers 16:3. What was the chief complaint of Korah and the men he assembled in the rebellion?

Read Numbers 16:12-14. Dathan and Abiram had a different complaint. What was it?

Korah, Dathan and Abiram were all seeking to elevate themselves rather than submitting to the leadership God had appointed for His people.

Dathan and Abiram were from the tribe of Reuben, and Reuben was the firstborn son of Jacob. According to the culture of that time, the firstborn son had position and authority. For this reason, the Reubenites may have felt that they (instead of Moses) should have been leaders among the Israelites.

Korah was a Levite in the clan of Kohath. (Numbers 16:1) All the Levites, including Kohath, were called to God's service, but only Aaron and his sons were appointed as priests.

In Leviticus 8-9, we read about how Moses consecrated Aaron and his sons for the priesthood according to God's commands. The consecration was done in front of the entire congregation and lasted for eight days.

Read about the conclusion of the consecration of Aaron and his sons in Leviticus 9:22-24. How did God make it clear to all the Israelites that He had appointed Aaron and his sons to this role?

Look back at what you learned on Day 5 of this study. What were the responsibilities of the Kohathites?

How did Korah's rebellion demonstrate discontentment with his appointed role? (Numbers 16:8-10)

Korah had assembled a rebellion against Moses and Aaron, but who was he ultimately rebelling against? (Numbers 16:11a)

The men who rebelled against God in Numbers 16 coveted roles that God, in His sovereignty and wisdom, had given to others. Their discontentment and covetousness had disastrous consequences. (vv. 31-35) In the New Testament, we are taught that the sin of Korah can serve as a cautionary tale for us as we seek to honor the Lord in the roles He's given to us. (Jude 11)

What are some of the roles God has given you right now in your family, workplace, church and community?

In which areas do you find yourself struggling with discontentment with your role or responsibilities? Are you tempted to covet a role God has given to someone else?

Paul writes in Ephesians 2:10 that God has prepared good works for us, and He's created us to do those good works. This truth can help us be content with the roles God has given to us in our current season of life. Rather than coveting what He's given to others, we can encourage each other as we walk in the good works God has prepared for us.

# DAY 20

---

**MAJOR MOMENT**: Aaron's atonement for the people's sin stopped a deadly plague.

At this point, we might start to wonder if the Israelites would ever learn a lesson from the previous rebellions. Although God gave them visible, tangible reminders of the consequences of sin, the Israelites continued to disobey. This is a great reminder of our need for Christ. We were also disobedient rebels until God transformed our hearts by His Spirit.

> In Numbers 16:36-40, what did God command Eleazar to do with the censers of the men who sinned by rebelling against Moses and Aaron's God-given authority?

> What purpose did the bronze altar covering serve for the people? (v. 40)

> What does this tell you about God's heart for His people and His desire to protect them?

> Read Numbers 16:41. How long did it take for the Israelites to start grumbling again?

When the people came against Moses and Aaron with false accusations, Moses didn't defend himself. The Lord came to Moses' defense and was ready to destroy the people. (Numbers 16:42-45) However, Moses once again interceded for the people by telling Aaron to atone for their sin. (Numbers 16:46)

What do you learn from the example of Moses and his repeated, undeserved compassion for the Israelites who kept grumbling against him?

Read Matthew 5:43-44 and Luke 23:34. What do you learn from Jesus' teaching and example about how to respond to the unfair actions or accusations of others?

Sin had a deadly effect on the Israelites, but when Aaron atoned for their sin, the plague God sent to judge them was stopped. The atonement was the dividing line between death and life. (Numbers 16:48)

And much like Aaron stood with the offering of incense and stopped the ravage of death tearing through God's people, Jesus offered Himself on the cross to free us from the power of sin and death. (Romans 5:18)

The cross of Jesus is the dividing line between death and life, and we are all on one side of that line or the other. Apart from Christ, we are unable to escape our sinful nature and the death our sin deserves. We either remain in our sin and deserve condemnation, or we repent and believe in Jesus. Those who are in Christ receive His gracious, free gift of grace and eternal life.

Have you received Christ's free gift of eternal life? If not, what questions do you have about Jesus, and how can you seek answers from the Bible, a local church or Christians you know?

Who do you know who is still dead in their sins and needs to hear the Good News of Jesus? Below, write a prayer for them and ask the Lord for an opportunity to share the life-giving news of what Jesus has done.

# WEEKEND REFLECTION
# + PRAYER

Do you ever feel like you deserve something better? Maybe you think you deserve the promised land, but you feel like one of the Israelite children stuck with 40 years in the wilderness. Feelings of entitlement lead to the discontentment, grumbling, unbelief and rebellion we saw in this week's passages.

As we learned from Romans 6:23, the only thing sinners like you and me deserve is death. While this truth is harsh, it sets the stage for the marvelous truth of God's mercy. Jesus took what we deserved and gave us the salvation we could never earn for ourselves. Jesus endured death; we enjoy life. Jesus experienced condemnation; we receive forgiveness and justification. As we keep our eyes trained on this gospel Truth, we can wait for our eternal home with contentment, peace and trust in our good Father.

**PRAYER:** Gracious Redeemer, thank You for the gift of Your grace and all the blessings I could never do enough to deserve. I confess I often feel entitled to more rather than being content with all You've given. Help me to grow in my understanding of the gift of Your salvation, and give me boldness to share the Good News with others. In Jesus' name, amen.

# WEEK FIVE

# DAY 21

**MAJOR MOMENT**: God confirmed Aaron's priesthood with a budding staff.

As we've seen in our last few days of study, the Israelites were exceedingly stubborn in their refusal to trust God and His plan. Even stunning displays of divine power and judgment didn't curb their grumbling. Today's reading begins with God giving instructions to Moses.

> Read Numbers 17:1-7. According to verse 5, what was the twofold purpose of God's experiment-like instructions with the staffs?

Biblical scholar Roy Gane makes an interesting point that this method of testing was both appropriate and symbolic because the Hebrew word for "staff" (*matteh*) can also be used for "tribe."[1] Each staff, or rod, was a literal representation of one of the tribes of Israel.

It's also significant to note that these staffs were pieces of wood picked up in the desert. While they may have been whittled and smoothed, maybe even decorated with carvings, the rods were dead wood.[2]

> Read Numbers 17:8-9, and explain in detail what Aaron's rod did overnight.

When have you ever seen a dead branch or wooden cane produce new growth? By God's power, Aaron's staff defied nature and became a budding, blossoming, fruit-bearing rod.

> Read Hebrews 5:1-6. What does verse 4 say about Aaron and the honor of being a high priest?

The budding staff proved God's authority to appoint leaders while also illustrating His power to bring life out of death. What a beautiful foreshadowing of our Savior's resurrection! And there is an interesting link between resurrection and the priesthood. Bear with me while we dig deeper to discover the connection.

The criteria for priesthood generally included two factors: <u>divine appointment</u> and <u>lineage through the tribe of Levi</u>. However, based on Hebrews 7:14, which tribe did Jesus descend from?

How then is Jesus qualified to be our High Priest? The author of Hebrews compared Jesus to another high priest called Melchizedek (introduced in Genesis 14:17-20), writing that Christ *"has become a priest, not on the basis of a* _____ *requirement concerning* _____ _____*, but by the power of an* _____ _____*"* (Hebrews 7:16).

I can't help but be stirred to wonder when I look at these parallels …

The <u>resurrected rod</u>
confirmed Aaron as <u>high priest</u>
to serve in the <u>earthly tabernacle</u>
on behalf of the <u>Israelites</u>.


The <u>resurrection of our Lord</u>
confirmed His role as <u>eternal High Priest</u>
to serve in the <u>*"holy places"*</u>
on behalf of <u>all humanity</u> (Hebrews 8:2).

Read Hebrews 4:14-16. What are the benefits and blessings for believers now that Jesus is our Great High Priest?

Read Numbers 17:12-13. The budding of Aaron's staff led the Israelites to develop a correct fear of approaching a holy God, but they lacked understanding of His purpose. God wanted them to have life, not death. As scholar Iain Duguid explains, "This blooming almond branch was a symbol of the certainty that the Lord would fulfill his promise of great blessing for his people through the gift of the priesthood."[3]

How do the truths in today's lesson impact your perception of God and your level of trust in His plan for you?

Aaron's Staff Buds

# DAY 22

**MAJOR MOMENT**: God explained the duties and privileges of priests and Levites.

The first word of today's passage is *"So"* (Numbers 18:1). When used as a conjunction, it means "therefore." So ... it's important to look back at the end of Chapter 17 to understand the point that follows in Chapter 18.

Let's recap the end of yesterday's passage. Read Numbers 17:12-13.

Who was speaking?

Whom were they speaking to?

What was the speakers' concern?

The Israelites finally understood they lacked the holiness needed to safely approach the tabernacle, but now they were consumed with fear and despair. So ... out of compassion and mercy for His people, God responded by outlining a new plan that offered some protection to the Israelites by placing responsibility (and potential divine judgment) upon Aaron and the tribe of Levi.

According to Numbers 18:1, who would *"bear iniquity connected with the sanctuary,"* and who specifically would pay the consequences for immoral behavior or wickedness connected with the priesthood?

Whereas the Levite priests were instructed to guard the interior of the tabernacle, the other Levites were given the responsibility to guard the exterior. (vv. 3-4) Instead of all of Israel, now the Levites would primarily be the ones to suffer God's judgment if there were trespassers. In this way, they were a gift to Israel. (v. 7) God's holy requirement for righteousness in order to approach Him remained and applied to individual trespassers; the risk of God's judgment on all of Israel remained a possibility, but the Levites were motivated to help protect God's people.

According to Numbers 18:5, why was it important for Aaron and his sons to *"keep guard over the sanctuary and over the altar"*?

How does this responsibility point to the work of Jesus, as it relates to the wrath of God?

I'm sure Aaron was relieved not to be alone in his ministry work.

How did God describe the Levites and the priesthood to Aaron in verses 6-7?

After laying out the high-stakes duties of the priests and Levites, God explained the rewards and privileges they would enjoy because of their special roles and risk-laden service.

Read Numbers 18:20b and fill in the blanks. The Lord told Aaron, *"I am your _____ and your _____ among the people of Israel."*

The Levites had the special advantage of being able to draw near to God.

*The Lord's presence is His greatest provision and our most profound privilege.*

The Levites were distinct from the other tribes in that they did not inherit any land, which was a tribe's livelihood. But God provides for His people, and He worked out a system of compensation for the Levites' service.

According to Numbers 18:21, what was the Levites' reward and inheritance, and where did it come from?

No one was exempt from the call to contribute to God the best of what they had. Even the Levites were instructed to present *"a tithe of the tithe"* to the Lord (Numbers 18:26).

How was the Israelites' obedience crucial to the ministry and livelihood of the priests and Levites?

How does tithing today impact a church or ministry's ability to operate and flourish?

Consider how you utilize your material assets, talents, time, etc. Beyond financial gifts, how are you currently dedicating the best of what you have to the Lord? What else could God be calling you to offer for His glory?

And the Lord said to Aaron, "You shall have no inheritance in their land, neither shall you have any portion among them. I am your portion and your inheritance among the people of Israel."

# DAY 23

**MAJOR MOMENT**: God prescribed laws for purification.

Today's passage details the specific laws God prescribed for sin offerings and the intricate purification process for those who were ritually unclean. Through close contact with death — since nearly everyone had been contaminated by the many deaths following Korah's rebellion — the Israelites had become ceremonially defiled and therefore couldn't approach God in worship until they completed a process of purification.

> In Numbers 19:2, what criteria did God give for selecting the sin offering?

The reddish color of the cow (along with the cedar and scarlet yarn mentioned in verse 6) hinted at the significance of blood as the means for atonement.

> Leviticus 17:11 explains that the blood represents the life of the animal. According to the rest of that verse, why is the blood significant?

> Numbers 19:10b specifies that the law was "a _____ statute for the people of Israel …" What do you think this means?

The cleansing process was not a one-and-done deal but a ritual to be repeated regularly. Why? God's standard of holiness never changes, but the status of the Israelites did change. They could not, on their own, remain spiritually "clean." Regular ceremonial cleansing and atonement would be necessary for the Israelites to remain in relationship with a holy God. The rituals foreshadowed the ultimate cleansing from sin that would come through the blood of Christ.

Read Hebrews 9:11-14 and complete the chart to see how Christ's atoning death forever changed the rituals prescribed for the Israelites.

| | Numbers 19 (before Christ) | Hebrews 9:11-14 (in Christ) |
|---|---|---|
| SIN OFFERING | Ashes of a blemish-free heifer (v. 9) | (v. 14) |
| PLACE | Outside the camp/the tent of meeting (v. 3) and toward the tent of meeting (v. 4) | (vv. 11, 24) |
| PURIFICATION | Purified the flesh (v. 9) | (v. 14) |
| EFFECTIVENESS | Temporary (v. 10) | (v. 12) |

In Numbers 19:11-22, additional cleansing laws were given for anyone who touched a deceased person, a human bone or even a grave. God demonstrated mercy by providing a way for His people to be purified so they could be in His presence.

Let's take a look at why death is associated with contamination and therefore offensive to God.

Read Romans 5:12. How did death come into the world?

1 Corinthians 15:22 says, *"For as in Adam all _____ , so also in Christ shall all be made _____ ."*

James 1:15 says, *"Then desire when it has conceived gives birth to _____ , and sin when it is fully grown brings forth _____ ."*

According to 1 Corinthians 15:26, *"The last enemy to be destroyed is _____ ."*

Sin, uncleanness and death cause separation from God because He is righteous, pure and the source of life.

But there's good news! What are we promised by the Apostle John in 1 John 1:9?
*"If we _____ our_____ , he is faithful and just to_____ us our _____ and to _____ us from all _____ ."*

We may have difficulty relating to the rituals and requirements in today's reading, but we have the opportunity to recognize the absoluteness of God's holiness and purity. We are also reminded, as Duguid expresses so well, that "by ourselves we are unfit to stand in the presence of a holy God."[4] Thankfully, in His mercy, God made a way. It is only because of the blood of Christ that we are washed clean of our sins and able to boldly draw near to the Lord.

---

**MAJOR MOMENT:** The new generation of Israelites departed for Canaan, but Moses and Aaron would not enter the promised land.

We're doing some time travel today! In Numbers 20, we jump forward *38 years* from Israel's rejection of the promised land and the announcement of God's judgment upon the older generation. After wandering in the wilderness for nearly four decades, the older generation of Israelites was mostly deceased, and the new generation departed from Kadesh toward Canaan.

In light of God's declaration in Numbers 14:29-31, how did this reality confirm that God is true to His word?

Chapter 20 begins and ends with the passing of Moses' siblings. We read in Numbers 20:1 that Miriam, who was a prophetess and Moses' protective big sister, (Exodus 15:20; Exodus 2:4-8) died and was buried in Kadesh. Numbers 20:22-29 records the death of Aaron, who, as we know, was Israel's high priest, Moses' brother and his partner in leading the Israelites.

I can't help but tear up when I envision Moses ceremoniously transferring Aaron's priestly garments to Aaron's son and successor, Eleazar, knowing he must soon say goodbye to Aaron.

We're given some more details about Aaron and his death in Numbers 33:37-39. What do you learn from these verses?

Based on Numbers 20:24, why wouldn't Aaron live to enter the promised land?

Now read Numbers 20:2-13. The account of this incident at the waters of Meribah is sandwiched between the deaths recorded in today's chapter.

What was the problem, and how did the younger generation of Israelites respond to this trial?

Even though dehydration was a legitimate concern, the younger generation clearly had not learned from their parents' mistakes. (Exodus 15:22-27)

According to Exodus 16:6-8, what had Moses taught the older generation about their grumbling when they first reached the desert?

Like their parents, this new generation of Israelites rose up against Moses with complaints and accusations. As Bible scholar Raymond Brown so clearly puts it, "Obsessed by what had been denied, they forgot what had been given."[5] Brown also reminds us of our own tendency: "Longing for what we want, we ignore what we have received."[6]

As Moses and Aaron often did in response to complaints from Israel, they sought the Lord's guidance. He told the two men to take a wooden staff, gather the people together and "_____ *the rock before their eyes to yield its water*" (Numbers 20:8a).

Based on Numbers 20:11, what did Moses *actually* do, and how was it different from God's command?

In addition to disobedience, Moses made another serious mistake. When he spoke to the Israelites in verse 10, to whom did he appear to give credit for the power to provide water ("*shall _____ bring water for you[?]*")?

Oh, Moses. God's humble servant had built a legacy of obedience. But on this occasion, Moses let his frustration and temper get the best of him (as we all can do) and handled the situation his own way. Moses' blunder revealed his flawed nature and the need for a greater and perfect Deliverer and Mediator... Jesus.

What was God's reason for denying Moses and Aaron the privilege of leading the new generation of Israelites into the promised land? (v. 12)

Think about situations in your own life where you have decided either to trust God or handle things your own way. What consequences have you experienced when you decided to handle things? What blessings have you received when you trusted God?

Before the chapter closes with Aaron's death, we also read that Israel's progress forward was halted by the king of Edom. Despite Israel's petition to pass through peacefully, the king denied them passage through his land, which was the most direct route to Canaan. This meant they would have to endure the inconvenience, extra time and physical toll of traveling out of their way and around the contentious nation.

Perhaps the Israelites had more growing up to do before God would position them for victory. Like Israel, we may not understand God's timing or the path He leads us to take, but God often uses detours for our development.

Looking back on a season of waiting, what invaluable lesson or truth did you learn in the process?

***God's timing is rarely predictable, but His promises are always dependable.***

**MAJOR MOMENT:** Israel received their first victory over the Canaanites.

After a period of grieving Aaron's death, the Israelites picked up and continued on their journey. They didn't travel far before meeting an obstacle.

Read Numbers 21:1-3. Who initiated the battle?

In a rare moment of faith and humility, the Israelites recognized the Lord as their source of strength and protection, and they pleaded for Him to grant them victory.

Read Deuteronomy 20:16-18. Why did it matter that Israel vowed to completely destroy the Canaanite cities?

The Israelites experienced their first victory over the Canaanites in Hormah, where the previous generation had been defeated almost 40 years earlier. Comparing the scenario in Numbers 21:1-3 with that in Numbers 14:36-45, what was the defining difference, which led to opposite results?

Israel's first victory over the Canaanites marked a turning point for God's people. But it wasn't long before Israel's trust in God's plan faltered yet again.

What was their punishment for complaining to Moses again about the lack of food and water? (Numbers 21:6)

In Numbers 21:7, the people who survived the snakes acknowledged their sin and repented. Consider for a moment what conditions in your day-to-day life are most likely to lead you to gripe. How can you combat an ungrateful heart or cynical mind?

In response to Moses' prayer, God instructed him to build a bronze snake as an antidote for the poisonous snake bites. (Numbers 21:7-9) According to a note in the *ESV Study Bible*, "The Hebrew term translated 'bronze' can also mean 'copper.'" And similar to what we learned in Chapter 19 about the significance of red objects, like the heifer, cedarwood and scarlet yarn, the "redness of copper suggested atonement."[7]

What does Jesus say in John 3:14 about Moses and the bronze snake?

Theologian Warren Wiersbe gives a helpful explanation for the connection: "But why should Moses make a model of a serpent, the very creature that was causing people to die? Because on the cross, Jesus became sin for us—the very thing that condemns people—and bore in His body that which brings spiritual death."[8] Just as those who suffered poisonous bites could look to the metal serpent for healing, all who look to Jesus and call upon His name will be saved. (Romans 10:13)

What an exciting development in Israel's journey! Later in Numbers 21, verses 10-20 summarize the route Israel traveled as they moved into the territory of the Amorites, and verses 21-35 detail the conquests of Heshbon and Bashan, with Israel securing victories. These wins increased the Israelites' confidence that they might truly conquer Canaan and possess "the land of milk and honey." The chapter closes with Israel possessing the whole region east of the Jordan River.

We've learned from the Israelites that repentance, obedience, gratitude and worship are vital to sustaining faith, both in times of victory and when life doesn't seem rosy or rewarding. How can you create or maintain habits of these spiritual practices in your life?

# WEEKEND REFLECTION + PRAYER

This week's readings were another powerful reminder of God's holiness and purity, and our failure to uphold these standards. Despite the Israelites' wickedness and disobedience, God's unfailing provision emerged from each chapter as a common theme. From a miraculous confirmation of God's authority and Aaron's priesthood to protection from His wrath, from tribal tithes supporting the Levites to purification rituals maintaining fellowship with God, from water gushing out of a rock to divine victory, God's ability and desire to care for His people were on full display.

My hope is that we will take time today to notice and appreciate the many ways God has provided for our needs and responded to our prayers. Through Jesus' death and resurrection, we have a Great High Priest who continually intercedes on our behalf. By His blood, we have been redeemed once and for all.

**PRAYER:** Lord, we recognize we're not so different from the Israelites. Our sin is abundant. But so is Your mercy and grace! Thank You, Jesus, that we are no longer condemned — because Your blood covers our every failure and cleanses us from guilt and shame. Lead us this week in pursuing holiness, and transform our hearts so we desire what's pure and noble and true. Help us to be content with what we have been given and to trust You for what we need. In Jesus' name, amen.

WEEK SIX

# DAY 26

**MAJOR MOMENT:** Balak summoned Balaam, a pagan seer, to curse Israel.

Our last lesson concluded with Israel's defeat of the Amorites. (Numbers 21:25) Though Israel was making progress toward claiming the promised land, Chapter 22 begins the account of their third and lengthy encampment on the plains of Moab; like their stays at Sinai and Kadesh, this season involved more lawgiving, rebellion, idolatry and military battles. You may be quite surprised, however, to find that today's passage involves bribery, angels and a talking donkey! Are you intrigued yet?

Let's dive in and read Numbers 22:1-6.

According to verse 4b, who was Balak?

Rather than rely on military strength, what was Balak's strategy to combat Israel? (vv. 4-6)

Balaam, son of Beor, was a pagan seer from Mesopotamia. He's somewhat of a perplexing character, coming across as an obedient, God-honoring prophet one moment and a manipulative charlatan the next.

Did Balaam seek the Lord's word regarding Balak's request? Who initiated his encounter with God in verse 9 and again in verse 20 (who "came" to whom)?

According to Numbers 22:12, why did God forbid Balaam from going to Moab and cursing the people of Israel?

What was Balaam's reason for refusing Balak's invitation? (v. 13)

Note that Balaam didn't give the whole truth. Had he informed the messengers of the fact that Israel couldn't be cursed because they were blessed, Balak might not have sent for Balaam again. Among many scholars, a common interpretation of Balaam's refusal is that he was "playing hard to get" and subtly negotiating for more money.

After Balak's second invitation, God gave Balaam permission to go with the princes of Moab, but on what condition? (v. 20)

We read in Numbers 22:22 that *"God's anger was kindled because he went ..."* Scholars commonly suggest that the meaning behind this phrase is not that God had changed His mind but that He knew Balaam's true motivation: presumably the money Balak was offering. God proceeded to reinforce His condition that the diviner was only to speak the words spoken to him by the Lord.

The humor and irony of the next verses are that the "seer" with "magical powers" was blind to the angel standing before him in the road, yet the donkey could not only see the angel, but suddenly the animal could speak!

When the Lord opened Balaam's eyes, what was his response? (v. 31)

We will learn more about Balaam in tomorrow's lesson, but what are your initial observations about this interesting man, particularly his moral principles?

The story in today's passage might seem far-fetched. But Raymond Brown reminds us of this great truth: "When God wants to announce great themes, influence multitudes, change lives and shape destinies, he will use whoever and whatever he wishes — a pagan king, a greedy soothsayer, even a voiceless donkey."[1]

When you consider the gospel story, what other surprising ways do you see God working to get the world's attention?

---

**MAJOR MOMENT**: Balaam delivered his first and second oracles.

At the end of yesterday's passage, Balaam was greeted by King Balak upon his arrival in Moab. The seer was up-front with his intentions, declaring he would only say the words God put in his mouth. (Numbers 22:38) You would think Balak might have asked for his money back after this confession, but he seemed to believe God would permit a curse on Israel if Balak could just appease Him with sacrifices and the right conditions.

> Read Numbers 23:1-12. In the first of three oracles, Balaam announced his purpose in Moab. To the Moabite king's dismay, he then proceeded to bless Israel rather than curse them.

> What does verse 8 communicate about the nature of God, even from a pagan's perspective?

What the Moabite king didn't know was that his plan had no possibility of succeeding because God had made a promise to Abraham in Genesis 12:1-3.

> According to those verses, what did God say would happen to those who rose up against Israel (the people of Abraham)?

Not only was Israel protected by God's blessing and covenant promise, but they were also bestowed with a specific purpose.

> In Exodus 19:6, what did God call Israel to be?

The literal meaning of "holy" is "set apart." Balaam's description of Israel in Numbers 23:9 as *a people dwelling alone* refers to Israel's identity as the chosen people, a nation set apart for God's glory.

To better understand Numbers 23:10, read Genesis 13:14-16 and Genesis 28:14.

Based on these verses, what does the *"dust of Jacob"* (Numbers 23:10) represent?

As we read yesterday, Balak took Balaam up to a high place, as it was considered helpful to have the targeted group in view when pronouncing a curse. And yet even seeing only *a fraction of the people* of Israel, Balaam found them too numerous to count (Numbers 22:41)!

Raymond Brown clearly summarizes Balaam's words thus far: "The seer's first oracle identified Israel's unassailable security, distinctive identity, unique heritage and ultimate destiny."[2]

Annoyed by the seer's words, Balak took Balaam to a different geographical spot and repeated a ritual of sacrifices. However, God's promise of protection and blessing for Israel was only reinforced in Balaam's second oracle: You'll find it in Numbers 23:18-24.

You might be familiar with the words of Numbers 23:19, but did you know this beautiful truth was spoken by a pagan seer? Take a moment to write out verse 19 below.

What do we learn about God's nature and character from this verse?

Balaam's second oracle highlighted God's faithfulness to His word as well as His presence with the Israelites. (Numbers 23:21) Wiersbe notes, "The first oracle pictured Israel as a chosen people because of the love of God, and the second oracle presents them as a conquering people because of the faithfulness of God."[3]

What aspect of God's nature do you most need to be reminded of today?

**MAJOR MOMENT:** Balaam delivered his third oracle.

Today's chapter opens with Balaam positioned to deliver a third blessing on Israel, much to the frustration of Balak, the king who wanted to curse God's people.

> Read Numbers 24:1-2.

> What did Balaam do differently this time?

The Spirit of God came over Balaam, and he uttered the third oracle, which we read in verses 3-9. Note that, while he couldn't see the angel of the Lord on his way to Moab, now his eyes were opened and he saw *"the vision of the Almighty"* (Numbers 24:4). He then proceeded to paint a glorious picture of Israel's future as a prosperous and powerful nation.

> What detail in the vision stands out to you most?

The story of Balak and Balaam paints the pagan seer in a somewhat positive light because God speaks through him, but other mentions of him in Scripture reveal a different perspective. Read the following verses and take note of what you learn about Balaam and his character.

> Deuteronomy 23:4-5

> Nehemiah 13:1-2

> 2 Peter 2:15

> Jude 11

> Revelation 2:14

Balaam is a prime example of the reality that not all who see or hear the Lord choose to follow Him. (Matthew 7:21-23)

A summary of Numbers 22-24 appears in Deuteronomy 23:3-6. According to verse 5 of the latter account, what did God do for His people, and why?

This story reminds me of what Joseph declared to his brothers in Genesis 50:20. What do his words teach us about the nature of God?

How have you seen Joseph's words in Genesis 50:20 play out in your own life?

How comforting it is to know that our God is sovereign! We can rest and rejoice in what we know to be true of the God we love and serve. Read the following verses and record what you learn specifically about the Lord.

Nehemiah 13:2

Proverbs 21:1

Romans 8:28

Before Balaam went back home, he gave a warning to Balak about a future ruler who would rise out of Israel and be victorious over all foes: *"I see him, but not now; I behold him, but not near: a star shall come out of Jacob, and a scepter shall rise out of Israel ... [and] shall exercise dominion ..."* (Numbers 24:17-19). While some of these prophecies were fulfilled in King David 300 years after the Israelites settled in Canaan, the oracles also spoke prophetically about the Messiah.

What does 1 Corinthians 15:25 say about Jesus?

How does Jesus describe himself in Revelation 22:16?

We must keep in mind that the Israelites had no idea about the potential attack being planned by Moab's king at the time of Balaam's prophecy. The stories and oracles eventually reached them and are recorded in this book of the Pentateuch, but let's not miss the fact that, while they camped at the base of the mountains, God was at work "behind the scenes" to guard and protect His people.

Let's close today by reading Psalm 121 and praising God for watching over us, night and day. Below, write one or two of your favorite verse(s) from Psalm 121.

# DAY 29

**MAJOR MOMENT**: Israel turned from God to worship Baal.

Numbers 25 opens with the Israelites living in Shittim, their final place of encampment before they crossed the Jordan. In stark contrast to the blessings spoken by Balaam, God's people entered into blatant sin and idolatry.

> Read verses 1-3. Seduced by the Moabite women, the Israelites began to do what at their invitation?

> According to Numbers 31:15-16, the Moabite women did this on the advice of whom?

Yesterday's passage ended with the statement that Balaam returned to his home. (Numbers 24:25) He may not have uttered curses on Israel, but we learned he wasn't necessarily a pious, God-fearing fellow.

> According to Revelation 2:14, what was Balaam doing behind the scenes?

The word *baal* is a term for "lord" or "master" and became a reference for various Canaanite gods. There were many baals, which is why the idol in this passage is referred to as "*Baal of Peor*" (Numbers 25:5).

It's true that the Moabite women were seducing the Israelite men. But the Israelites were not without warning about the dangers of mingling with those who lived in the land they were taking possession of.

Read Exodus 34:10-16. What were the potential snares God said would result from Israel making treaties with or marrying the Moabites?

The consequences of God's wrath toward the Israelites' perversion were severe. The evil had to be atoned for in order to turn the Lord's anger away from His chosen but rebellious nation.

According to Numbers 25:9, how many died in the plague against the Israelites?

Based on Numbers 25:6-8, what stopped the plague?

What reason did God give for establishing a covenant of peace with Phinehas, Aaron's grandson? (vv. 12-13)

Paul referenced this incident in 1 Corinthians 10:8 when he warned the Corinthians about sexual immorality. It is also cited in Psalm 106, which gives a summary of Israel's dramatic history.

Read Psalm 106:28-31. What was credited to Phinehas?

While we have Psalm 106 in front of us, look specifically at verses 13-39. Take a few minutes to make a list of the many different ways Israel sinned against God. The NIV translation may be most helpful for this exercise. I'll get us started.

God's people ...

Forgot what God had done. (v. 13)

Did not wait for God's counsel. (v. 13)

Gave in to their craving. (v. 14)

Finished? You should have at least 25 transgressions listed. The vastness of the sins is a bit shocking, isn't it?

Now I'm going to ask you to do something hard ... Go back and underline or highlight any sins that you're similarly guilty of.

And now with (hopefully) contrite hearts, let's read the awe-inspiring and grace-filled words of Psalm 106:44-45. These words applied to Israel. And my friend, they're true also for you and me. Even with Israel's long history of missteps, God never gave up on them. No matter how much we stumble in our faith, God will lead us faithfully to repentance and forgiveness in Christ, and ultimately to the promised land of heaven.

# DAY 30

---

**MAJOR MOMENT**: God commanded Moses and Eleazar to take a census of Israel's new generation.

The events in today's reading mark a significant step in Israel's history as a new era dawned for the nation. Now that 40 years had passed and the old generation was deceased, it was time for the Israelites' transition from wandering in the wilderness to settling down in Canaan — the promised land. Read Numbers 26:1-4 and note the key details.

To whom was God speaking?

Where were God's people at this time?

When did this happen?

What instructions were given?

The primary focus of the first census was to count the number of men able to fight. While this was also a factor in the second census, God revealed another purpose to Moses in Numbers 26:53. What was His response following the tally of the people of Israel?

*"Among these the _____ shall be _____ for _____ according to the number of names."*

The second census included not just total tribal numbers but also details about the specific clans within each tribe. Just as in the first census, the Levites were listed separately because they had been given the responsibility of the priesthood, and the Lord Himself, rather than land, was their inheritance. (Numbers 26:62)

Using the new census information, Moses was instructed to portion out the land to the tribes by size and by lot. This would prevent conflict over who got what land because casting lots was an unbiased method of determining a decision, somewhat like drawing straws or flipping a coin. The Lord, in His sovereignty, could direct the outcomes as He saw fit.

What does the census and process of land allocation reveal about God's nature?

How does God's involvement in the details affect your perception of how He sees you? How does it affect your faith in His plans for you?

Among those who were counted in the second census, how many people were listed? (Numbers 26:51)

How does that tally compare to the first census, recorded in Numbers 1:46?

The lists were very similar in number but almost completely different in people listed. By God's grace and provision, the people of Israel had not dwindled during their 40 years of wandering. An entire generation passed away, but a new generation had risen up.

> Besides Moses, who were the only two remaining from the original men counted in Numbers 1? (Numbers 26:65)

> Flip back to Numbers 14:5-10. As a reminder, how did Caleb and Joshua respond to the bad reports of their fellow spies and the rebellion of God's people?

As a reward for their faith and leadership, Caleb and Joshua were granted exemption from God's punishment on the rebellious Israelites. The final verse of today's chapter confirms that God was true to His word in preserving their lives so they could enter the promised land.

The NASB translation of 2 Chronicles 16:9a tells us, *"For the eyes of the LORD roam throughout the earth, so that He may strongly support those whose heart is completely His."*

> Similarly, God described Caleb in Numbers 14:24 (ESV) as his *"servant"* and one who *"has a _____ _____ and has _____ me _____ ..."*

> Based on Caleb's example, what do you think it looks like to follow God fully, to give your heart completely to Him?

# WEEKEND REFLECTION + PRAYER

This week we've seen that God's plans prevail regardless of who or what comes against Him. Contrary to what Balak believed, God cannot be manipulated, conned or controlled. He selected Israel to be the nation through which He would bring the blessing of salvation to all people, and not even Israel's fickle faith and apostasy could make Him retract His promise. The consequences for those who turned away to worship Baal of Peor were severe, but in His faithfulness to His word, God preserved the nation of Israel as a whole.

The lesson for all of us is that we are just as susceptible to idolatry and sinful pursuits. God will never forsake us or remove the promise of our salvation through Christ, but such love and grace should stir us to respond in joyful obedience.

**PRAYER:** Heavenly Father, I praise You for Your unmatched power and authority. You are worthy of all my attention and adoration, and I long to be consistent and faithful in my relationship with You. Please give me wisdom to avoid distractions, and strength to fight temptations. Help me to remember that, because I'm a child of God, I am more than a conqueror through Christ. In Jesus' name, amen.

NUMBERS

---

**MAJOR MOMENT**: God commissioned Joshua to be Moses' successor.

Today's chapter opens with the story of Zelophehad's daughters, descendants of Joseph. We saw their names recorded in Numbers 26:33 as part of the second census, and we now discover the reason for them being identified in the listings. Read Numbers 27:1-4 and note the details.

> To whom did the daughters present their case? (v. 2)

> What was their plight? (v. 3)

> What solution did they propose? (v. 4)

Traditionally, daughters did not receive an inheritance from their father but were instead given a dowry upon their marriage. A man's land and possessions were divided up among his sons, and this was how the family name was carried forth. Without sons, a father's estate would be passed on to his brothers or closest male relatives, and his name would essentially be forgotten.

> What was the Lord's response when Moses brought the case before Him, and what new rule did He institute? (Numbers 27:5-11)

> What does this story communicate to you about God's value of women and His sense of fairness?

Also looking toward the future inheritance of Israel, verses 12-23 mark an emotional and significant turning point in Israel's story. Up until this point, Moses had served as God's appointed deliverer, leader, advocate and mediator for the people of God. The Lord informed His humble servant that his time on earth was nearing its end and he would need to climb a mountain to die, just like his brother Aaron.

Because of his and Aaron's disobedience in the wilderness of Zin, Moses had forfeited his right to cross into the promised land. But before his last breath, what would God allow Moses to do? (v. 12)

Deuteronomy 34:1-4 provides a few details about this special moment. Wiersbe notes, "Though he wasn't allowed to go in himself, Moses invested the closing weeks of his life in preparing the new generation to enter Canaan and claim the land God promised to give them."[1]

Read Numbers 27:16-17.

What did Moses request of the Lord?

What do his concerns reveal about his heart and his sense of responsibility?

According to Numbers 27:18, whom did God appoint as Moses' successor?

Joshua was assisted by Eleazar the priest, who used the Urim and Thummim to determine God's will for the people. These were objects, possibly in the form of sticks or stones, like dice that revealed answers of "yes" or "no" from God. (Nehemiah 7:65) We read in Exodus 28 that whenever Aaron entered into the Lord's presence he was required to place the Urim (meaning "lights") and Thummim (meaning "perfections") in the pocket of his priestly chestpiece to carry over his heart. (Exodus 28:30)

You're probably thinking what I'm thinking ... *How incredible to be able to seek God's guidance and receive a concrete, visible answer!* This practice, however, had a specific purpose for Israel at that time. Today, through study of God's Word and sensitivity to the Holy Spirit, the Lord helps us discern the way we should go.

In Numbers 27:22-23, Moses publicly commissioned Joshua to lead Israel. Let's read Deuteronomy 31:1-8, which recounts the same event, for some additional details.

> Moses emphasized that Joshua had no reason to fear because he had two major advantages: God's promise (to take possession of the land) and His presence. Friends, we, too, have the gifts of God's promises and presence. Whatever concern might be weighing on you today, consider and write down some ways His promises and presence make it possible to walk forward in faith rather than in fear.

---

**MAJOR MOMENT**: God gave specific instructions about public sacrifices and offerings.

Before Israel could conquer and claim the promised land, God commanded Moses to instruct His people on exactly what living as a holy nation would entail. Once they settled in their new homeland, worship through sacrifices and offerings would play a key role.

A phrase you'll see repeated throughout today's chapter is *"a pleasing aroma"* (vv. 2, 6, 8, 13, etc.) related to the sacrifices offered to the Lord.

> Read Genesis 8:20-21.
> What impact did Noah's burnt offering have on the Lord?

The Hebrew word for "pleasing" (*nikhoakh*) means "soothing, delightful, pleasant." The aroma of the burnt offerings, and the worship that produced this aroma, soothed God's anger toward sin. Scholar Warren Wiersbe points out that "Each of the offerings had a different purpose to fulfill, but the ultimate goal was to please the Lord and delight His heart."[2]

God prescribed a pattern of worship with a calendar of rituals. These sacrifices were offered in public worship and made on behalf of the whole nation by the priest.

**DAILY OFFERINGS** (Numbers 28:1-8)

*Timing*
> Based on Numbers 28:4, when were the regular offerings of a lamb made? (Not every person was to supply this daily, but the people were to take turns willingly supplying this as needed.)

*Purpose*
Wiersbe explains that "the burnt offerings typified total dedication to the Lord."[3]

*Contemporary significance*

> Romans 12:1 says we offer our "_____ as a living _____, holy and acceptable to God, which is [our] spiritual _____."

> According to Romans 12:2, what does it look like to be living sacrifices, to dedicate ourselves fully to the Lord?

## SABBATH OFFERINGS (vv. 9-10)

### Timing
Each week on the Sabbath, morning and evening.

### Purpose
Read Exodus 31:15-17. Why did God want the Israelites to observe the Sabbath?

### Contemporary significance
As Brown explains, "Israel's worship pattern gave special prominence to this weekly occasion for worship, necessary rest from the pressures of everyday work, and essential family time."[4] Humanity's need for these blessings remains today. Resting weekly is a picture of the eternal rest we have received in Christ. (Hebrews 4:9-11)

## MONTHLY OFFERINGS (vv. 11-15)

### Timing
On the first day of every month. These sacrifices were also called "new moon" offerings because the Israelites followed a lunar calendar.

### Purpose
In addition to the burnt offerings, the priests were instructed to sacrifice a male goat as a sin offering. (Numbers 28:15) What does Leviticus 4 explain about sin offerings? (See Leviticus 4:20, 26, 31 and 35.)

By incorporating sin offerings into the monthly rituals, God ensured Israel could make a fresh start each month with their sin atoned for and forgiven.

### Contemporary significance
Regularly coming before God to confess and repent for our sins helps us remember our need for forgiveness and for a Savior. How can you make repentance a priority in your life?

## ANNUAL OFFERINGS (vv. 16-31)

God provides instructions for a total of five annual events in Numbers 28 and 29. Let's look at the two events discussed in today's reading.

### THE PASSOVER (Numbers 28:16-25)

*Timing*

According to Numbers 28:16, when was the Lord's Passover to be celebrated?

*Purpose*

The Passover celebrated Israel's deliverance from Egypt, when the Lord passed over the houses of the children of Israel that were marked with the blood of a sacrificial lamb. (Exodus 12)

For seven days following the Passover, the Israelites were instructed to make additional sacrifices and remove all traces of yeast (symbolic of sin) from their homes as part of the Feast of Unleavened Bread. (Exodus 13:3; Deuteronomy 16:3)

*Contemporary significance*

Read 1 Corinthians 5:6-8. How is Christ the fulfillment of the Passover?

### THE FEAST OF WEEKS (Numbers 28:26-31)

*Timing*

Based on Leviticus 23:15-16, where on the calendar did this feast fall?

This feast was later known as Pentecost because "fifty" in Greek is pentēkonta.

### *Purpose*
The Israelites brought the firstfruits of their crops as a celebration of thanksgiving for God's gracious and generous provision. (Exodus 23:16) This feast also marked the beginning of the wheat harvest.

### *Contemporary significance*
Today, Christians recognize Pentecost as the day when believers were filled with the Holy Spirit as promised by Jesus. (Acts 1:4-5; Acts 2:1-40)

Many of the offerings God commanded were tied to remembrance of His faithfulness, protection, guidance and provision.

How has recalling God's past faithfulness to you strengthened your faith in Him in the present?

---

**MAJOR MOMENT**: God continued to outline a calendar of public sacrifices and pertinent laws.

Yesterday, we looked at two of five annual celebrations commanded by the Lord through Moses to the people of Israel. Today we will look at the remaining three: the Feast of Trumpets, the Day of Atonement and the Feast of Booths.

## THE FEAST OF TRUMPETS (Numbers 29:1-6)

### *Timing*
> When was this annual event to occur? (v. 1)

The seventh month was considered to be the holiest month of the year.

### *Purpose*
The sounding of trumpets was used to signal gatherings, alarms and battles. Trumpets were also blown over the sacrifices and offerings as a symbolic plea for God to remember His people. (Numbers 10:1-10)

### *Contemporary significance*
> Read 1 Thessalonians 4:16-18. What is the significance of the trumpet sound Christians are waiting to hear?

## THE DAY OF ATONEMENT (Numbers 29:7-11)

### *Timing*
> This holy day occurred on the 10th day of the seventh month, after which other feast? (Hint: We just studied it above.)

### *Purpose*
The Day of Atonement was an annual occasion for the Israelites to be assured of complete cleansing and forgiveness for all their sins. The people were instructed to gather for worship, fast and rest from work. Leviticus 16 describes this day in great detail.

This was the only day of the entire year that the high priest was permitted to enter the Holy of Holies in the temple, and he was required to make atonement for himself, his household and the whole community of Israel. (Leviticus 16:17)

### Contemporary significance
The Day of Atonement foreshadowed the day when Jesus would die on the cross to become a sacrifice of atonement for the sins of all humanity.

## THE FEAST OF BOOTHS OR FEAST OF TABERNACLES (Numbers 29:12-39)

### Timing
On the 15th day of the seventh month (five days after the Day of Atonement).

> How long was this festival to last? (v. 12)

### Purpose
During this week, the Israelites would live in temporary "booths" or tents to remember and celebrate God's presence, provision and protection for His people during their 40 years in the wilderness.

### Contemporary significance
Just as God provided care for His people as He led them toward the promised land, God provides everything we need as we wait for Jesus to return and usher believers eternally into the Kingdom of God.

It's difficult for the modern-day Church to understand what a significant role the ancient sacrificial system played in the lives of the Israelites. The requirements for offerings were costly, as Wiersbe helps us understand: "Totally apart from the sacrifices that the people brought in their own personal worship, and the great number of lambs slain at Passover, each year the priests offered 113 bulls, 32 rams, and 1,086 lambs!"[5] The rituals and celebrations were also time-consuming but necessary.

And yet the instructions Moses delivered to Israel surely sparked some hope.

> If God expected the Israelites to provide offerings of food, drink, grain and livestock throughout each year, what could they surmise about their future livelihood in Canaan and the land's condition?

Read Hebrews 9:22. Why did the law require the Israelites to make sacrifices and offerings?

But according to Hebrews 10 (which quotes Psalm 40:6-8), the offerings and sacrifices could *"never take away sins"* (Hebrews 10:11) or truly and fully please the Lord.

Rituals were a way for Israel to remain in relationship with God *"until the fullness of time"* came to send forth His Son into the world to be our Savior (Galatians 4:4).

Write out the incredible news recorded in Hebrews 10:10, and underline the phrase *"once for all."* Imagine how the Israelites would have reacted to such an announcement!

---

**MAJOR MOMENT**: God taught Israel about the obligation of vows.

In our passage today, Moses addressed the importance of keeping one's word. Gordon Wenham's commentary helps us understand why this topic would naturally flow from the previous chapter on sacrifices. He writes, "... vows were usually sealed with a sacrifice; and, when the prayer was answered, another sacrifice would be offered."[6]

The Hebrew word for "vow" (*neder*) meant promising the Lord to perform a certain deed in the future. It could also mean abstaining from a behavior prohibited by the Lord. In Numbers 30, Moses specifically discusses differences between vows made by women and men.

Let's break down the various scenarios.

***Men and Vows*** (Numbers 30:1-2)
Men were expected to follow through on their vows without exception.

***Women and Vows Before Marriage*** (Numbers 30:3-5)
Before marriage, in ancient Israel, women lived under their fathers' authority.

> Therefore, what could happen if a father disapproved of his daughter's vow? (v. 5)

***Married Women and Vows*** (Numbers 30:6-8; Numbers 30:10-15)
A woman's husband had the authority to void her vows, even ones she made before marriage. Such broken promises were forgiven by God. If a husband knew of his wife's vow or pledge and said nothing, his silence signified approval of her vows.

> According to verse 15, if a husband nullified his wife's vows after the day he heard of them, rather than immediately, who paid the penalty for the canceled vow?

***Widows and Female Divorcees*** (Numbers 30:9)
If no longer under the authority of a father or husband, a woman's vow was binding.

If you find it difficult to think of a woman's vows being subject to her father's or husband's approval, consider the following point from Wiersbe about "the importance of authority and subordination in society and in the home. While all people are created equal before God and the law, there are still levels of authority and responsibility that must be respected."[7] When God established fathers and husbands as the head of the household, His purpose was (and is) to create order and maintain peace and harmony in marriages and families. (Ephesians 5:22-23; Ephesians 6:1-3)

God cares about the sanctity of vows because honesty and reliability are foundational to healthy relationships. Notice that when Moses discussed vows, he also warned against *"any thoughtless utterance"* that uses binding language (Numbers 30:6).

What does Proverbs 20:25 say about careless words?

What are some examples of thoughtless promises we might make to God but fail to uphold? How can we be more mindful about the words we say?

Read Ecclesiastes 5:2-7. These wise words are great to use as a guided prayer. Which verse resonates most with you?

---

**MAJOR MOMENT**: God declared vengeance on Midian.

Today's reading begins with a reminder that Moses would soon no longer be leading Israel. Before climbing the mountain for his final moments, he had one more assignment from God to carry out.

According to Numbers 31:1-2, what was Moses' task?

God was punishing Midian for leading His people into sin during the Baal-Peor episode. (Numbers 25) As a reminder, what did we learn in Genesis 12:1-3 about those who curse Israel?

Moses was not pleased when the army returned, though they were victorious. Based on Numbers 31:15-16, what was he angry about? (Remember, we mentioned the Midianite woman on Day 29.)

Following Israel's war against Midian, the process of ritual purification is brought up again in Numbers 31:19-24. Bible scholar Gordon Wenham shares this insight: "These purification rules reminded Israel that the death of one's fellow men was a catastrophic disruption of God's creation, even though in some cases it was the Creator himself who demanded the execution of the sinner."[8]

What did the commanders do in response to God's protection of every single Israelite soldier? (vv. 48-50)

Read Exodus 30:11-16. Who was instructed to give atonement money following the census in these verses, and what was it used for?

The commanders gave above and beyond their required atonement money as a gift to the Lord for His faithfulness and the victory He secured for them.

In these verses we see a celebration of a military victory of the Lord's army, but we must be very careful not to confuse today's reading with contemporary arguments in favor of killing for religious causes. Brown emphasizes that "we should leave vengeance to God. This narrative about the destruction of the Midianites is descriptive, not prescriptive. It relates how Israel acted, under divine instruction, at a specific moment of time and for a particular purpose."[9]

Another scholar, Wiersbe, adds: "The church has no mandate from God to engage in 'holy wars' (John 18:10-11, 36) because our enemies aren't flesh and blood (Eph. 6:10ff.) and our weapons are spiritual (2 Cor. 10:1-6). The sword of the Spirit is the only sword we use to advance the cause of Christ (Eph. 6:17-18)."[10]

How does what you've learned in our study of Numbers help you read other parts of the Bible that might be challenging to understand?

# WEEKEND REFLECTION + PRAYER

Our readings this week covered more instructions and laws to prepare the Israelites for holy living when they got settled in the promised land. God was to be the focus and the center of their existence. The teaching of these principles conveyed hope that the Israelites would indeed cross into Canaan and enjoy a fruitful and fertile land.

Jesus longs for us to experience abundant life, but it's only possible when we are living God's way. We are all accountable to Him. Regularly repenting for our sins, celebrating Christ's ultimate sacrifice on our behalf and recalling God's goodness are ways we can realign our priorities with the Lord's and discover the joy and peace that can only be found in Him.

**PRAYER:** Lord, I praise You that Your Word is trustworthy and dependable. Forgive me for all the times I've rejected your guidance and chosen my own path. You alone know what is best. As the Israelites learned through their festivals and offerings, teach me to depend on You when I'm in need and to praise Your name when I'm in a season of plenty. Help my words and actions be a reflection of Your love and Truth. In Jesus' name, amen.

# WEEK EIGHT

# DAY 36

---

**MAJOR MOMENT**: The tribes of Reuben and Gad settled in Transjordan.

Today's reading adds a little plot twist to Israel's quest toward the promised land. The tribes of Reuben and Gad assessed the Transjordan — territory that Israel took possession of when God led them to defeat Sihon and Og (Numbers 21) — and concluded that the land was suitable for their *"very great number of livestock"* (Numbers 32:1). In fact, it seemed so ideal that Reuben and Gad preferred to stay in that area east of the Jordan River and allow the rest of Israel to cross into the promised land without them. (Numbers 32:3-5)

Moses responded to their proposition with a rather fierce scolding.

> Read Numbers 32:6-7. In addition to accusing the men of not doing their part in Israel's conquest of Canaan, Moses expressed concern that their decision would do what?

> Moses then compared their proposal to what event in Israel's history? (vv. 9-13)

The two tribes modified their argument and proposed that they should have the opportunity to build cities for their women and children, and pens for their livestock. And then they declared they would be ready to join the other tribes in conquering Canaan and securing the promised land. Not only would they fight, but they wouldn't go back to their homes until every tribe had possession of its own territory. (v. 18)

Moses agreed, but what were the conditions he set in Numbers 32:20-23?

What are the last five words of Moses' command in verse 24?

After studying the importance of keeping vows and being dependable in Chapter 30, we better understand the gravity of Moses' words.

We read about the outcome of this situation in Joshua 22. What happens in Joshua 22:1-6?

Note the commandment in Joshua 22:5, given to them by Joshua. Fill in the blanks below using the NIV translation.

*"But be very _____ to keep the commandment and the law that Moses the _____ of the LORD gave you: to _____ the LORD your God, to _____ in obedience to him, to _____ his commands, to _____ _____ to him and to _____ him with all your _____ and all your _____."*

God allowed the tribes of Reuben and Gad to remain outside of Canaan. But their hesitation to inhabit God's promised land is not necessarily an example to follow. Sometimes we may forfeit God's best for us by choosing to live by sight and not by faith. I think of times I've been hesitant to take action because I was unsure of what lay ahead. I chose to settle for the comfort of familiarity rather than experience the joy of discovering God's provision.

What are some comforts potentially holding you back from obedience to God?

What are some actions you could take to obey God wholeheartedly?

# DAY 37

---

**MAJOR MOMENT:** Moses recounted the stages of Israel's journey.

Our reading today provides a record of Israel's journey from Egypt to Canaan. Starting off from Rameses (Egypt) and ending at the plains of Moab, God's people camped at 40 places over the course of 40 years. God instructed Moses to keep a record of their travels, perhaps as a testimony to God's provision and sovereignty.

To help us recall the important moments and displays of God's faithfulness in Israel's journey, let's glance at the passages and chapters cited below.

| NUMBERS 33 RECAP | STAGES OF ISRAEL'S JOURNEY | KEY EVENTS |
|:---:|:---:|:---:|
| VV. 3-4 | Leaving Egypt (Exodus 12:1-13:22) | The Passover (Exodus 12) |
| VV. 5-8 | Rameses through the Red Sea to Marah (Exodus 12:37-15:26) | Passing through the Red Sea (Exodus 14) |
| VV. 9-15 | Marah to Mount Sinai (Exodus 15:23-19:2) | Bread from heaven (Exodus 15) Water from a rock (Exodus 17) |
| VV. 16-36 | Sinai to Kadesh (Exodus 12:11-20:1) | Failed entrance into Canaan (Numbers 13-14) |
| VV. 36-37 | 30 years of wandering (Numbers 14:1-20:21) | Korah's rebellion (Numbers 16) The budding of Aaron's staff (Numbers 17) Water from another rock (Numbers 20) |
| VV. 37-49 | Kadesh to the plains of Moab (Numbers 20:22-27:23) | The bronze snake (Numbers 21) Balak and Balaam (Numbers 22) Moab seduces Israel (Numbers 25) The Second Census (Numbers 26) Joshua commissioned to succeed Moses (Numbers 27) |

What have you learned about God and about Israel from these key events?

It's hard to know exactly why this passage is included in Numbers, but Wenham suggests, "Since Moses' great achievements took place at the stations mentioned, this list serves as a sort of obituary for him, and this is an appropriate place in Numbers to insert an obituary."[1] Brown suggests that recalling the past events would "inspire confidence, issue warnings, and encourage trust for the days ahead" for Israel.[2]

Have you ever taken time to record a timeline of important moments or stages in your spiritual growth? Just as God's hand can be traced in the details of Israel's journey, we're better able to see how God has worked in our own lives when we reflect on past events.

Write down several personal instances when God's love, provision or faithfulness were particularly evident to you.

We see from today's chapter that our faith benefits from both looking back at God's faithfulness and looking forward toward His promises. Following the recounting of Israel's journey, the Lord reassured Moses that the Israelites would indeed take possession of the promised land. Some of the information in Numbers 33:50-56 may seem familiar because it was also recorded in Chapter 26 after the census. In Chapter 33 God added some important instructions:

Once the Israelites crossed the Jordan River, what were they to do before settling down into their new territories? (v. 52)

Keeping in mind Israel's history of being negatively influenced by pagan cultures, why would the destruction in verse 52 have been such a critical commandment to obey?

In Numbers 33:55-56, what did God say would happen if the Israelites failed to drive out the inhabitants from the land?

God's Word provides wisdom, and some of it comes through warnings. A little spoiler alert ... The Israelites eventually faced consequences for their failure to heed God's warnings once they moved into the promised land.

In what ways does God's Word reassure you that He has our best and eternal interests at heart?

**MAJOR MOMENT**: God outlined the boundaries of the land of Canaan.

As the Israelites prepared to enter the land of Canaan, they must have felt an overwhelming combination of emotions: excitement, awe, maybe a little bit of apprehension. At the end of Numbers 33, God had just reassured the Israelites that they would take possession of the land because He had given it to them.

What was God's promise to Abraham in Genesis 17:8?

While the land of Canaan had been promised generations before, the exact boundaries had never been defined. If the Israelites were to follow God's command of driving out the inhabitants, they needed to know exactly where the borders of their territory began and ended.

Once the borders were defined, it was time for the tribes to be given their particular territories within Canaan. As we recall from Numbers 32, the tribes of Reuben and Gad, as well as the half-tribe of Manasseh, had already received their inheritance.

What does Numbers 34:15 say about their territory?

Based on Numbers 34:17, who was given the responsibility of gathering the remaining 10 tribal chiefs for the distribution of land, and what were the roles of these two men at this point in Israel's history?

1. Name: _____ — Role:

2. Name: _____ — Role:

Read Numbers 34:18-28 and fill in the chart with corresponding details about the tribes settling west of the Jordan.

| SCRIPTURE REFERENCE IN NUMBERS 34 | TRIBAL CHIEF | TRIBAL NAME |
|---|---|---|
| V. 19 | Caleb, son of Jephunneh | Judah |
| V. 20 | | |
| V. 21 | | |
| V. 22 | | |
| V. 23 | | (of Joseph) |
| V. 24 | | (of Joseph) |
| V. 25 | | |
| V. 26 | | |
| V. 27 | | |
| V. 28 | | |

According to Numbers 34:29, *"These are the men whom the LORD commanded to _____ the _____ for the people of _____ in the _____ of _____."*

I can't help but wonder if the tribal chiefs felt any pride, envy or curiosity as they received their territories. Did they compare size, location or agricultural potential? The human tendency is to look beyond what we've been given and yearn for what we do not have. When I struggle with comparison or doubting God's purposes, the psalmist's words of contentment in Psalm 16 provide comfort and a fresh perspective.

Write Psalm 16:5-6 below.

Some translations of Numbers 34 incorporate the word "boundary" when describing the lines. The boundaries God draws in our lives, like He drew in the lives of the Israelites and the promised land, may not make sense to us, but they are part of His perfectly appointed plan. What might seem like limits could actually be divine boundaries of grace. No matter where we are or what we feel we lack, we have the everlasting promise of God's presence and peace.

What boundaries in your life are you grateful for today?

# DAY 39

---

**MAJOR MOMENT**: The Levites were given some cities in which to live.

Following the distribution of land to the 10 tribes in Chapter 34, the Lord instructed Moses to provide the Levites (the priestly tribe) with cities to dwell in and pasturelands for their livestock. You can find a detailed account in Joshua 21.

Read Numbers 35:6-7.

How many cities in total were the Levites to receive?

From that total, how many cities were to serve the purpose of being a refuge?

According to Numbers 35:8, the cities were to be given from *"the possession of the _____ of _____"* and *"in _____ to the inheritance"* of each tribe.

Because every other tribe was required to give up some of their land, the tribe of Levi was spread out across Canaan.

How does this fulfill the Lord's curse upon Levi and his brother Simeon in Genesis 49:5-7 as a consequence for their slaughtering of Shechem's inhabitants?

The tribe of Levi was shown grace — they were scattered but yet remained a distinct group with the sacred responsibility of the priesthood. In his commentary, Duguid also makes this excellent point:

"The Levites' absence of an earthly inheritance was always intended to force them to recognize that the Lord himself was their inheritance. They had houses to live in and enough land to graze their livestock (v. 3), but they never had enough to settle down and become altogether comfortable. In this, the Levites were a sign to Israel: they were to be a group within Israel whose eyes were to be firmly fixed on the heavenly inheritance, pointing others in the same direction."[3]

This doesn't mean living comfortably is necessarily wrong for us as God's people. But how can earthly comfort sometimes become a stumbling block in our faith?

Awareness of what we have in Christ can lead us to recognize the world's inability to fully satisfy us.

What hope does Jesus give believers in John 14:1-3?

According to Philippians 3:20, where is our citizenship?

Our future hope is heaven, but our present reality is life on earth. Throughout biblical history, God has provided laws and guidelines to help humanity live as uprightly and peacefully as possible. Let's take a quick look at how He instructed the Israelites to handle matters of murder and manslaughter in Numbers 35:9-34.

Read Numbers 35:9-15. Who were the cities of refuge for?

Verses 16-21 give examples of murder with intent to injure or kill. What was the penalty for the killer in these scenarios?

Verses 22-29 provided a protocol for someone who unintentionally took another person's life.

What were the legal punishments and reprieves for a manslayer?

What must happen in order for the manslayer to return to his own land? (v. 28)

Note that either situation — murder or manslaughter — required atonement for the killing. This requirement was met by the execution of the murderer or (in manslaughter cases) the death of the high priest.

How does this statute foreshadow the gospel of Christ?

What does Numbers 35:31-32 say about a ransom?

Christ gave *"his life as a ransom for many"* and provided the ultimate sacrifice of atonement to cover any and all sin (Mark 10:45). Jesus is our refuge we can run to!

Let's finish today by writing a prayer of thanksgiving and praise for God's grace and mercy.

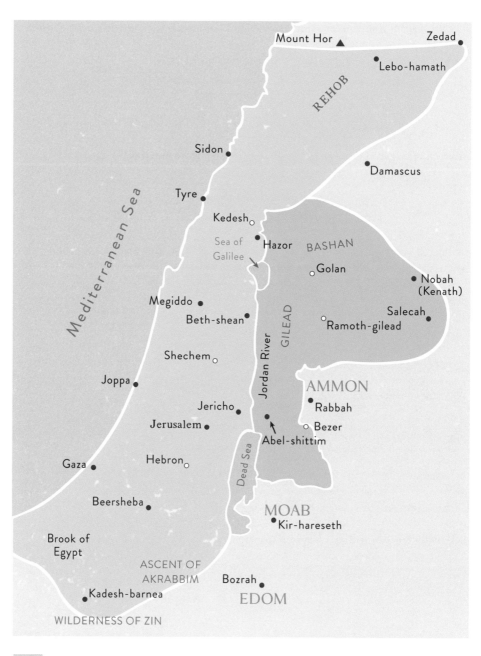

# BOUNDARIES OF THE PROMISED LAND

Mount Hor ▲

Zedad

Lebo-hamath

REHOB

Sidon

Damascus

Tyre

Kedesh ○

Sea of Galilee

Hazor

BASHAN

Golan ○

Nobah (Kenath)

Megiddo

Beth-shean

GILEAD

Salecah

Ramoth-gilead ○

Mediterranean Sea

Shechem ○

Jordan River

Joppa

AMMON

Jericho

Rabbah

Jerusalem

Bezer ○

Abel-shittim

Gaza

Hebron ○

Dead Sea

Beersheba

MOAB

Kir-hareseth

Brook of Egypt

ASCENT OF AKRABBIM

Bozrah

Kadesh-barnea

EDOM

WILDERNESS OF ZIN

Extent of the promised land according to Numbers 34

○ Designated city of refuge

Land occupied by Reuben, Gad, and Manasseh

# DAY 40

---

**MAJOR MOMENT**: God instituted a marriage rule to preserve each tribe's inheritance.

It's our last day of study, and if you're looking for a neat and tidy wrap-up of Israel's story, you'll have to keep reading … Deuteronomy is your next destination. Today's reading begins with some family business.

According to Numbers 36:1, who appeared before Moses and the chiefs?

What was their concern? (vv. 2-4)

God's response and solution was that the daughters of Zelophehad had to marry within their tribe. This rule, stated in verse 7, is repeated in verse 9 to emphasize its importance. And the daughters' obedience is recorded in verse 10.

As we read Numbers 36:13, the very last verse of the book of Numbers, we might feel like the story has come to an abrupt end or, if nothing else, a conclusion that is … anticlimactic. But maybe there's more there. Let's flip back to Numbers 27, where we read about the request of Zelophehad's daughters.

Glancing back at Numbers 27:12-14, what is recorded directly after the daughters' story and the new inheritance rule? Who was the Lord speaking to?

In the same manner, following another law related to Zelophehad's daughters, in Numbers 36:13 our focus is brought back to Moses — God's devoted spokesperson and servant leader.

> Drawing from the details in Numbers 36:13, where was Moses as he passed along these commandments and rules to Israel?

Moses and the people of Israel were on the threshold of the promised land; all they had to do was cross the Jordan River. For 40 years, Moses had faithfully delivered God's commandments to the people of Israel and helped prepare them for this impending and anticipated stage in their journey. As you might recall from Chapter 27, God commanded Moses to climb the mountain where he would die, and Moses did indeed obey God's word, but the account of his death is found at the end of the book of Deuteronomy.

> At this point in Moses' life, I imagine him being weary and run-down. It would seem that four decades of leading, teaching, mediating, praying, writing and traveling would have taken a huge physical, emotional and spiritual toll on this elderly man. And yet how is Moses described in Deuteronomy 34:7?

The book of Numbers ends with a declaration that the Lord instituted the commands and rules through Moses. The final words of Numbers play out in my mind like a movie scene … the camera zooming in for a closeup of Moses as he stands alone and gazes ahead toward Jericho through perhaps tear-filled eyes, knowing his work of preparing Israel for entry into Canaan is almost done. I envision a smile of contentment spreading across his face as he imagines the Israelites stepping into a new land and experiencing the wonder and fulfilled promises of their mighty God.

The conclusion of Numbers is a reminder that the wilderness is not the end of the story. God has a remarkable future in store for His people, and just as He was faithful to bring His chosen nation into the promised land, we can trust Him to bring us, His beloved children, into eternal glory.

What do Revelation 21:2 and 22:1-3 say about the dwelling place God has prepared for those who follow Him?

When we experience seasons of wandering or feeling lost, when we are thirsty for more but fail to turn to the source of Living Water, when we know where we're heading but feel restless as we wait for God to "green light" our step forward ... these are times when we recall what we've learned from the Israelites.

We repent of our sin and allow the blood of Jesus to cleanse our hearts.

We clear out the idols in our lives and worship only the Lord our God.

We guard our mouths and follow through on our words.

We hold up testimonies of God's past provision and hold tightly to His promises.

We confidently claim our inheritance and surround ourselves with the family of God.

We determine to persevere through the desert and
anticipate the glory of the *"city that is to come"* (Hebrews 13:14).

# NUMBERS
*in review*

## AUTHOR:

Moses

## GENRE:

Historical narrative (with portions of law)

## SETTING/KEY PLACES:

The wilderness — specifically three areas where Israel
encamped: Sinai (Chapters 1-10), Kadesh (Chapters 13-19)
and the plains of Moab (Chapters 22-36)

## TIME PERIOD:

Circa 1446/1260 B.C.

## PURPOSE:

To record Israel's season of wandering in the wilderness during their journey from Mount Sinai to the borders of Canaan and their preparation for entry into the promised land

## KEY FEATURES:

Moses, Miriam, Aaron, Eleazar, Korah, Dathan, Abiram, Joshua, Caleb, Balak, Balaam, the daughters of Zelophehad

## KEY VERSES:

Numbers 14:20-24, *"Then the LORD said, 'I have pardoned, according to your word. But truly, as I live, and as all the earth shall be filled with the glory of the LORD, none of the men who have seen my glory and my signs that I did in Egypt and in the wilderness, and yet have put me to the test these ten times and have not obeyed my voice, shall see the land that I swore to give to their fathers. And none of those who despised me shall see it. But my servant Caleb, because he has a different spirit and has followed me fully, I will bring into the land into which he went, and his descendants shall possess it.'"*

Numbers 14:11, *" And the LORD said to Moses, 'How long will this people despise me? And how long will they not believe in me, in spite of all the signs that I have done among them?'"*

## KEY THEMES:

God's presence, protection, provision and purity; Israel's unbelief and rebellion; the gradual fulfillment of God's covenant promise to Israel's patriarchs

# WEEKEND REFLECTION + PRAYER

Over the last eight weeks, we've had the opportunity to explore an important part of salvation history as God's redemptive plan continued to unfold through the Israelites' story. Through the rebellion and wandering of the older generation, we saw evidence of God's faithful provision and merciful grace. In the preparation of the new generation to possess the promised land, we observed the Lord's great attention to detail. From daily offerings and worship gatherings to inheritance laws and family protocols, God instructed His people on what to do and how, when and where to do it in order to live as a nation set apart for His glory.

Just as He longed to be a daily, integral part of Israelite life, God desires to be the center of our lives today, tomorrow and always. Not just when we're at a crossroads and need direction or when we're in a moment of crisis and call out for help. He cares about the way we talk, work, rest, socialize, give and serve. It matters to Him when we're hungry, thirsty, tired and feeling lost. And when we're satisfied, content and obedient. When we allow Him to lead us, we may not always feel like we're moving forward. But arrival at our final and glorious destination is assured. And His presence with us every step of the way is guaranteed.

**PRAYER:** Lord, teach me to live by faith rather than by sight. I know You love me, and I trust You to do whatever is necessary to sanctify me. Help me to embrace every delay, setback, boundary or act of discipline, knowing that it has been filtered through Your sovereign hands and allowed into my life for my good and Your glory. I fully surrender my will to You. In Jesus' name, amen.

# END NOTES

## INTRODUCTION

[1] Brown, Raymond. *The Message of Numbers: Journey to the Promised Land.* The Bible Speaks Today, edited by Alec Motyer and Derek Tidball. Nottingham, England: Inter-Varsity Press, 2002. p. 16.

[2] Brown, Raymond. *The Message of Numbers: Journey to the Promised Land.* The Bible Speaks Today, edited by Alec Motyer and Derek Tidball. Nottingham, England: Inter-Varsity Press, 2002. p. 16.

[3] Brown, Raymond. *The Message of Numbers: Journey to the Promised Land.* The Bible Speaks Today, edited by Alec Motyer and Derek Tidball. Nottingham, England: Inter-Varsity Press, 2002. p. 18.

## WEEK 1

### Day 1

[1] Brown, Raymond. *The Message of Numbers: Journey to the Promised Land.* The Bible Speaks Today, edited by Alec Motyer and Derek Tidball. Nottingham, England: Inter-Varsity Press, 2002. p. 27.

[2] Duguid, Iain M. *Numbers: God's Presence in the Wilderness.* Preaching the Word, edited by R. Kent Hughes. Wheaton, IL: Crossway, 2006. p. 30.

### Day 2

[3] Duguid, Iain M. *Numbers: God's Presence in the Wilderness.* Preaching the Word, edited by R. Kent Hughes. Wheaton, IL: Crossway, 2006. p. 46.

### Day 3

[4] Duguid, Iain M. *Numbers: God's Presence in the Wilderness.* Preaching the Word, edited by R. Kent Hughes. Wheaton, IL: Crossway, 2006. p. 36.

### Day 4

[5] Brown, Raymond. *The Message of Numbers: Journey to the Promised Land.* The Bible Speaks Today, edited by Alec Motyer and Derek Tidball. Nottingham, England: Inter-Varsity Press, 2002. p. 37.

## WEEK 2

### Day 6

[1] Massey, Ken. "Restitution." *Holman Illustrated Bible Dictionary*, edited by Chad Brand, et al. Nashville, TN: Holman Bible Publishers, 2003. p. 1379–1380.

[2] Gane, Roy. *Leviticus, Numbers.* The NIV Application Commentary. Grand Rapids, MI: Zondervan, 2004. p. 525–526.

### Day 7

[3] Duguid, Iain M. *Numbers: God's Presence in the Wilderness.* Preaching the Word, edited by R. Kent Hughes. Wheaton, IL: Crossway, 2006. p. 81.

[4] Duguid, Iain M. *Numbers: God's Presence in the Wilderness.* Preaching the Word, edited by R. Kent Hughes. Wheaton, IL: Crossway, 2006. p. 77.

[5] Duguid, Iain M. *Numbers: God's Presence in the Wilderness.* Preaching the Word, edited by R. Kent Hughes. Wheaton, IL: Crossway, 2006. p. 82.

# END NOTES

**Day 8**

[6] Sproul, R.C. "Jesus Became a Curse for Us." Ligionier.org, 2 April 2021. www.ligonier.org/posts/supreme-malediction-jesus-became-curse. Accessed 5 October 2021.

**Day 10**

[7] Crossway Bibles. *The ESV Study Bible*. Wheaton, IL: Crossway Bibles, 2008. p. 250.

[8] Duguid, Iain M. *Numbers: God's Presence in the Wilderness*. Preaching the Word, edited by R. Kent Hughes. Wheaton, IL: Crossway, 2006. p. 109.

## WEEK 3

**Day 14**

[1] Gane, Roy. Leviticus, Numbers. The NIV Application Commentary. Grand Rapids, MI: Zondervan, 2004. p. 590.

[2] Duguid, Iain M. *Numbers: God's Presence in the Wilderness*. Preaching the Word, edited by R. Kent Hughes. Wheaton, IL: Crossway, 2006. p. 164.

**Day 15**

[3] Crossway Bibles. *The ESV Study Bible*. Wheaton, IL: Crossway Bibles, 2008. p. 285.

## WEEK 4

**Day 16**

[1] Brown, Raymond. *The Message of Numbers: Journey to the Promised Land*. The Bible Speaks Today, edited by Alec Motyer and Derek Tidball. Nottingham, England: Inter-Varsity Press, 2002. p. 121.

[2] Thompson, J. William and Butler, Trent C.

"Intercession." *Holman Illustrated Bible Dictionary*, edited by Chad Brand, et al. Nashville, TN: Holman Bible Publishers, 2003. p. 810-11.

**Day 17**

[3] Duguid, Iain M. *Numbers: God's Presence in the Wilderness*. Preaching the Word, edited by R. Kent Hughes. Wheaton, IL: Crossway, 2006. p. 176.

**Day 18**

[4] Gane, Roy. Leviticus, Numbers. The NIV Application Commentary. Grand Rapids, MI: Zondervan, 2004. p. 619.

[5] Duguid, Iain M. *Numbers: God's Presence in the Wilderness*. Preaching the Word, edited by R. Kent Hughes. Wheaton, IL: Crossway, 2006. p. 184.

[6] Brown, Raymond. *The Message of Numbers: Journey to the Promised Land*. The Bible Speaks Today, edited by Alec Motyer and Derek Tidball. Nottingham, England: Inter-Varsity Press, 2002. p. 139.

[7] Crossway Bibles. *The ESV Study Bible*. Wheaton, IL: Crossway Bibles, 2008. p. 290.

## WEEK 5

**Day 21**

[1] Gane, Roy. Leviticus, Numbers. The NIV Application Commentary. Grand Rapids, MI: Zondervan, 2004. p. 644.

[2] McGee, Vernon J. Genesis through Deuteronomy. Thru the Bible. Nashville, TN: Thomas Nelson, 1981. p. 497.

# END NOTES

[3] Duguid, Iain M. *Numbers: God's Presence in the Wilderness.* Preaching the Word, edited by R. Kent Hughes. Wheaton, IL: Crossway, 2006. p. 214.

## Day 23

[4] Duguid, Iain M. *Numbers: God's Presence in the Wilderness.* Preaching the Word, edited by R. Kent Hughes. Wheaton, IL: Crossway, 2006. p. 214.

## Day 24

[5] Brown, Raymond. *The Message of Numbers: Journey to the Promised Land.* The Bible Speaks Today, edited by Alec Motyer and Derek Tidball. Nottingham, England: Inter-Varsity Press, 2002. p. 177.

[6] Brown, Raymond. *The Message of Numbers: Journey to the Promised Land.* The Bible Speaks Today, edited by Alec Motyer and Derek Tidball. Nottingham, England: Inter-Varsity Press, 2002. p. 177.

## Day 25

[7] Crossway Bibles. *The ESV Study Bible.* Wheaton, IL: Crossway Bibles, 2008. p. 299.

[8] Wiersbe, Warren W. *Be Counted: Living a Life that Counts for God.* OT Commentary Numbers. Colorado Springs, CO: David C. Cook, 1999. p. 117.

## WEEK 6

### Day 26

[1] Brown, Raymond. *The Message of Numbers: Journey to the Promised Land.* The Bible Speaks Today, edited by Alec Motyer and Derek Tidball. Nottingham, England: Inter-Varsity Press, 2002. p. 210.

## Day 27

[2] Brown, Raymond. *The Message of Numbers: Journey to the Promised Land.* The Bible Speaks Today, edited by Alec Motyer and Derek Tidball. Nottingham, England: Inter-Varsity Press, 2002. p. 212.

[3] Wiersbe, Warren W. *Be Counted: Living a Life that Counts for God.* OT Commentary Numbers. Colorado Springs, CO: David C. Cook, 1999. p. 134.

## WEEK 7

### Day 31

[1] Wiersbe, Warren W. *Be Counted: Living a Life that Counts for God.* OT Commentary Numbers. Colorado Springs, CO: David C. Cook, 1999. p. 153.

### Day 32

[2] Wiersbe, Warren W. *Be Counted: Living a Life that Counts for God.* OT Commentary Numbers. Colorado Springs, CO: David C. Cook, 1999. p. 159.

[3] Wiersbe, Warren W. *Be Counted: Living a Life that Counts for God.* OT Commentary Numbers. Colorado Springs, CO: David C. Cook, 1999. p. 159.

[4] Wiersbe, Warren W. *Be Counted: Living a Life that Counts for God.* OT Commentary Numbers. Colorado Springs, CO: David C. Cook, 1999. p. 159.

# END NOTES

### Day 33

[5] Wiersbe, Warren W. *Be Counted: Living a Life that Counts for God*. OT Commentary Numbers. Colorado Springs, CO: David C. Cook, 1999. p. 162.

### Day 34

[6] Wenham, Gordon, J. *Numbers*. Old Testament Guides. Sheffield, United Kingdom: Sheffield Academic Press, 1997. p.206

[7] Wiersbe, Warren W. *Be Counted: Living a Life that Counts for God*. OT Commentary Numbers. Colorado Springs, CO: David C. Cook, 1999. p. 167.

### Day 35

[8] Wenham, Gordon J. *Numbers*. Tyndale Old Testament Commentaries. Downers Grover, IL: Inter-varsity Press, 1981. p. 236-237.

[9] Brown, Raymond. *The Message of Numbers: Journey to the Promised Land*. The Bible Speaks Today, edited by Alec Motyer and Derek Tidball. Nottingham, England: Inter-Varsity Press, 2002. p. 275.

[10] Wiersbe, Warren W. *Be Counted: Living a Life that Counts for God*. OT Commentary Numbers. Colorado Springs, CO: David C. Cook, 1999. p. 168.

## WEEK 8

### Day 37

[1] Wenham, Gordon J. *Numbers*. Tyndale Old Testament Commentaries. Downers Grover, IL: Inter-varsity Press, 1981. p. 242.

[2] Brown, Raymond. *The Message of Numbers: Journey to the Promised Land*. The Bible Speaks Today, edited by Alec Motyer and Derek Tidball. Nottingham, England: Inter-Varsity Press, 2002. p. 292.

### Day 39

[3] Duguid, Iain M. *Numbers: God's Presence in the Wilderness*. Preaching the Word, edited by R. Kent Hughes. Wheaton, IL: Crossway, 2006. p. 357.

# Answer Key for Day 11:

| FIRST MONTH OF THE SECOND YEAR | | SECOND MONTH OF THE SECOND YEAR | |
|---|---|---|---|
| First day of the month | 14th day of the month | First day of the month | 14th day of the month |
| Exodus 40:16-17<br>Moses set up<br>the tabernacle.<br><br>Numbers 7:1-3<br>The people brought<br>offerings.<br><br>Numbers 9:15<br>The cloud covered the<br>tabernacle. | Numbers 9:1-5<br>The people celebrated<br>the Passover. | Numbers 1:1-2<br>God commanded Moses<br>to take a census. | Numbers 9:9-11<br>The unclean people<br>celebrated the Passover. |

# IN CASE YOU WERE WONDERING

Sometimes there is more to understanding Scripture than originally meets the eye. That's why our team wanted to provide you with additional information on some of the most popular verses from Numbers.

*"The LORD bless you and keep you; the LORD make his face to shine upon you and be gracious to you; the LORD lift up his countenance upon you and give you peace."* (Numbers 6:24-26)

The beauty of these verses lies in God's method of communication and the magnitude of the message.

God gave these words to Moses to give to Aaron to give to the people. Moses and Aaron were leaders but not the ultimate Leader. The people were conditioned to listen to and follow the direction of the priests. But here, God wanted to make sure His people remembered that the priests were only messengers. God is the Deliverer of the promise.

When God said He would bless them, (v. 24) He used the Hebrew word *Barak*, which means "kneel before," indicating God's coming near, His presence with His people. The Israelites could look around and see many who were blessed with material things, but only God's chosen people could be blessed with God's presence.

God emphasizes His personal relationship and His desire to come close; to guard and guide; to care for; and of course, as the presence of the living God always does, to bring peace.

*Cheryl Dale*

*"On the day that the tabernacle was set up, the cloud covered the tabernacle, the tent of the testimony. And at evening it was over the tabernacle like the appearance of fire until morning. So it was always: the cloud covered it by day and the appearance of fire by night."* (Numbers 9:15-16)

The tabernacle was God's dwelling place in Israel, His home, His tent pitched right in the center of the Israelite camp. (Numbers 2) He expected their lives to revolve around Him, not the other way around. He desired relationship with them, but He was not a "sidekick"; He was their sovereign Lord. As the tabernacle represented His home, the cloud and the fire reminded the people that He was at home.

This was His permanent residence, not a timeshare. He was always there — day and night. The cloud in the day and the fire at night were visible reminders of this reality — a comfort, a call to holiness and a source of help during the journey.

This image would become flesh when Christ came and tabernacled among us, (John 1:14) foreshadowing the even greater reality of Christ in us — the hope of glory (Colossians 1:27) — and the Holy Spirit coming to dwell in us as His temple. (1 Corinthians 6:19)

*Vera Christian*

*"And I will come down and talk with you there. And I will take some of the Spirit that is on you and put it on them, and they shall bear the burden of the people with you, so that you may not bear it yourself alone."* (Numbers 11:17)

God expresses great compassion and understanding for Moses' situation in this verse. First, God came. He saw the discouragement and the weariness and met Moses right where he stood. Second, we know God fully equipped Moses for the job, but still, when Moses felt overwhelmed, God understood. We, too, can trust God fully but still have days when we feel we can't go on.

God always provides. He met Moses' need by sharing with others some of the Holy Spirit power Moses had been given, so they could share in the care of the people. God had equipped Moses, but Moses no longer needed to do it alone.

We never need to do it alone. (Isaiah 41:10) God will always come with what we need right when we need it.

*Cheryl Dale*

*"And he said, 'Hear my words: If there is a prophet among you, I the LORD make myself known to him in a vision; I speak with him in a dream. Not so with my servant Moses. He is faithful in all my house. With him I speak mouth to mouth, clearly, and not in riddles, and he beholds the form of the LORD. Why then were you not afraid to speak against my servant Moses?'"* (Numbers 12:6-8)

In these verses, God reaffirms Moses' leadership after Aaron and Miriam challenged his calling by essentially asking, "What's so special about Moses?"

When God says he spoke to Moses *"mouth to mouth"* (some translations say "face to face"), God is not implying Moses saw His full glory. In Exodus 33 Moses asked to see God's glory, and God responded, *"I will make all my goodness pass before you … [But,] you cannot see my face, for man shall not see me and live"* (vv. 19-20).

The phrase *"mouth to mouth"* is a figure of speech that affirms the personal interaction and unhindered intimacy Moses experienced with God as God spoke with him directly and clearly. Numbers 12:7 tells us God saw Moses as *"faithful in all my house."* Moses' character matched his calling.

*Donna Jones*

*"The LORD is slow to anger and abounding in steadfast love, forgiving iniquity and transgression, but he will by no means clear the guilty, visiting the iniquity of the fathers on the children, to the third and the fourth generation."* (Numbers 14:18)

The Israelites had received reports from 10 of the spies who surveyed their promised land, and although it was as God said, only two spies believed Israel could take the land. (Numbers 13) Once hopelessness set in, the Israelites began to make plans to appoint a new leader to lead them back to Egypt. (Numbers 14)

God desired to strike them all down and start afresh with Moses. Moses interceded for Israel; he reminded God of His own words in Numbers 14:18. But because Israel lacked faith to claim the promised land, their children and grandchildren would continue to wander in the wilderness.

Our sins affect others. Just as God's punishment — the death of the unbelieving Israelites — was felt for generations, our parents' sins are not our sins, but we may suffer the repercussions of their actions or inaction for generations. God forgives our iniquities, but that does not mean we will escape all chastisement or consequences.

*Gina Duke*

**"On the next day Moses went into the tent of the testimony, and behold, the staff of Aaron for the house of Levi had sprouted and put forth buds and produced blossoms, and it bore ripe almonds."**
(Numbers 17:8)

God said *"the staff of the man whom I choose shall sprout"* (Numbers 17:5a). A dead branch, severed from trunk and root, sprouting life was a miracle within itself. But the working of God was more than just a sprout. He produced each stage of growth on this barren shaft of wood: buds, blossoms and ripe almonds. He made possible the impossible.

The Hebrew word for this common staple, the almond, comes from *shaqad*, meaning "wake" or "watchful," and the almond is a symbol of spring, renewal and hope. Almonds are the first to wake from winter with buds in January, followed by blossoms through March and harvest in July/August. By the power of God, a long growing season was condensed into one night to publicly display His authority in choosing the priestly leadership to watch over His wayward, grumbling people. A miracle that only God could perform was initiated in the very place where Aaron would serve Him.

*Sharon Bollinger*

**"And the LORD said to Aaron, 'You shall have no inheritance in their land, neither shall you have any portion among them. I am your portion and your inheritance among the people of Israel.'"**
(Numbers 18:20)

God promised His people He would deliver them from Egypt and give them their own land as an inheritance. After centuries of slavery and decades of wandering, God's people would now have a place to call their own — to settle down, raise their families and earn a living for generations to come. However, because service in the tabernacle required his full attention, Aaron, the high priest of Israel, wouldn't have been able to tend land had he received any.

At first glance, Aaron appears to be missing out, but in reality, he was gaining something better than land: God Himself. Even though he wouldn't have land to cultivate, God would provide for Aaron and his descendants through the tithes of the other tribes. Therefore, in this way, Aaron could be satisfied, knowing that the Lord was his inheritance, better than any earthly possession.

*Nora Tatina*

*"These are the waters of Meribah, where the people of Israel quarreled with the LORD, and through them, he showed himself holy."* (Numbers 20:13)

This verse is the conclusion of events that took place in Kadesh. (Numbers 20:2-12) The name "Meribah" was given to the waters in Kadesh due to how the Israelites acted in a time of lack. The congregation used sinfully combative words toward Moses instead of trusting in the Lord to provide. Their striving with Moses was as if they were striving with the Lord Himself since Moses was His representative.

But in response to the Lord's instruction, Moses reacted with anger and misrepresented the Lord, so He reproved Moses by not allowing him to enter the promised land. However, the Lord still *"showed himself holy"* by providing his people with an ample supply of water for them and their livestock.

The Lord showed Himself holy, not to condemn, judge or destroy them but to provide for them. The flow of water was the flow of pure love for His people, proving the Lord faithful to keep His promises.

*Christy Moore*

*"So Moses made a bronze serpent and set it on a pole. And if a serpent bit anyone, he would look at the bronze serpent and live."* (Number 21:9)

This metallic snake fashioned by Moses was made of *nechosheth*, a Hebrew word meaning bronze or copper. The area the Isaelites were passing through at this point was filled with copper mines and likely provided the materials needed — a strategic and yet profound provision from God.

Bronze throughout the Bible is symbolic of God's righteous judgment. We see items of bronze in the courtyard of the tabernacle, the bronze altar and the basin representing atonement and the cleansing of sin. (Exodus 27; Exodus 30:17-21)

As Moses lifted up this bronze serpent in the desert sun, and as light reflected from its burnished form, the people were prompted to look. Not just to glance but to behold, perceive and understand God's mighty power to save.

This nehushtan pole that took on the very image of the problem was now offering the cure. God was present to His people in the middle of evil, if only they would behold Him. His offer of salvation was revealed in a bronze snake, a symbol of life, not death. A true foreshadowing of things to come in the person of Jesus.

*Jill Boyd*

*"God is not man, that he should lie, or a son of man, that he should change his mind. Has he said, and will he not do it? Or has he spoken, and will he not fulfill it?"* (Numbers 23:19)

This verse carries the authority of the Lord speaking to Balaam to deliver His words to Balak, a pagan king.

The Lord gave Balak a command in verse 18 to rise and hear and to give his full attention to the character of the Lord. The Lord also called Balak the *"son of Zippor"* to acknowledge that He knew him (v. 18). Verse 19 confirms the full capacity of the Lord's character and attributes.

The Lord, who is set apart as holy, spoke His blessings and promises over Israel on many occasions. This passage confirms that His divine guarantee to bless His people will not change due to human agendas. God never forgets His very own words, so when trials and problems arise, we know He will strengthen us. We can rest in knowing that what flowed from His lips to our hearts cannot be altered but will be sustained through His truthfulness and faithfulness. His promises and blessings are irrevocable.

*Christy Moore*

# LEADER GUIDE

We appreciate your willingness to invite friends to join you as you journey through this First 5 study guide. It's our prayer that this Leader Guide equips you to lead more confidently and effectively as you study God's Word together.

## TIPS ON LEADING:

### PREPARE.
Reach out to your group and let them know you're excited to begin and you're praying for them. Confirm participants have their books. Confirm the time, place and location (coffee shop, church, house, Facebook, Zoom) where you will meet. Invite participants to read the background content in the first few pages of the study guide to provide a good foundation for the study.

### PRAY.
Set aside time to pray for the participants in your group.

### CONNECT CONSISTENTLY.
Be consistent in the day and time you meet. Honor participants' schedules by starting and ending on time. Invite them to make study days a priority through prompt, faithful attendance.

### SHARE.
Invite everyone in the group to participate and share in discussion. Especially in the beginning, be vulnerable and share what God is teaching you. Participants will follow your lead. Create a safe study environment by asking participants to hold in confidence everything shared during study time.

### LISTEN.
Let participants answer questions first. Don't be afraid of silence. Sometimes they need a moment to gain the courage to speak up. Listen and give eye contact as each participant shares. Engage and ask follow-up questions where appropriate. This ensures every participant feels valued and encouraged.

Be on the alert for participants who consistently dominate discussion. Find a way to gently interrupt, thank them for their thoughts and ask if anyone else would like to share.

Be sensitive to other participants. Invite those who have been quiet into the discussion, especially if you feel they have experience or knowledge that will add value.

Respect each participant's viewpoint. However, if their words are hurtful or go against Scripture, ask questions rather than argue or criticize (for example, "How did you come to that conclusion?" or "Is there a verse you found that helped you come to that conclusion?"). This avoids embarrassing and/or offending the participant.

## STAY ON TOPIC.

Stay on topic. Study group is time set apart to study the Bible. It is not a prayer group or a support group. Do your best to keep the discussion focused on the questions and scriptures at hand and on what the Holy Spirit is teaching and leading. When personal concerns arise, discuss what is appropriate and then move on. A good option is to gently interrupt and lift a short prayer, in the moment, for the person sharing and then move to the next question. If someone has a deep personal need, invite the participant to share her need with you after group time and decide how to proceed from there … mentoring, counseling, etc.

## FIRST WEEK:

Build community in your group. Invite participants to introduce and share something about themselves and share why they joined this First 5 study. Maybe ask what they hope to gain from the study, and revisit those answers at the end of the study.

## EACH WEEK:

Review each day's content and questions ahead of the day your group meets, including any special content added to deepen your study.

Prayerfully choose questions and/or special content on which you'd like to focus.

Close with prayer (either choose one person to close in prayer or, if time allows, ask for prayer requests). You may also want to invite participants to share what spoke most to their hearts that week, if time allows.

## PRAYER:

*Father, thank You for the privilege and honor of leading people through this First 5 study. Thank You for allowing me to be a vessel to help draw others closer to You through Your living, active, penetrating, life-transforming Word. Place Your holy hand upon me as I lead, and anoint me for Your service. As my group meets each week, open my ears and eyes to hear Your voice as I study and pray. Make my heart tender to the hurts and needs of those in my group. Give me the words to speak and the scriptures and questions to focus on. May each person in my group experience You in personal and powerful ways, and may our lives never be the same after this time we will spend together with You. Holy Spirit, move in our midst and do mighty works that only You can do. Finally, help me point study participants to You and You alone and bring glory and honor and praise to You and Your precious Son, Jesus. I ask this in Jesus' name, amen.*

**Adapt these tips to fit your group and how you meet (in person group, Zoom group or Facebook group).

# NOTES

# NOTES

# NOTES

# NOTES

# NOTES

# NOTES

# NOTES

# NOTES

# NOTES

# NOTES

# NOTES

A STUDY of the
BOOK of MATTHEW

# A BETTER WAY:

*How* JESUS' LIFE *Guides Us to* PEACE
*in a World That Steals* OUR SANITY

**Available (October) 2022 at p31bookstore.com**